AQUINAS'S
Summa

Background, Structure, & Reception

Jean-Pierre Torrell, O.P.

AQUINAS'S
Summa

Background, Structure, & Reception

Translated by
Benedict M. Guevin, O.S.B.

The Catholic University of America Press
Washington, D.C.

The paper used in this publication meets the minimum requirements of
American National Standards for Information Science—Permanence of
Paper for Printed Library materials, ANSI Z39.48–1984.

∞

Library of Congress Cataloging-in-Publication Data

Torrell, Jean-Pierre.

[Somme de theologie de saint Thomas d'Aquin. English]

Aquinas's Summa : background, structure, and reception / Jean-Pierre
Torrell ; translated by Benedict M. Guevin.— 1st ed.

p. cm.

Includes bibliographical references and index.

ISBN 13: 978-0-8132-1398-9 (pbk. : alk. paper)

ISBN 10: 0-8132-1398-3 (pbk. : alk. paper)

1. Thomas, Aquinas, Saint, 1225?–1274. Summa theologica.

2. Theology, Doctrinal.   3. Catholic Church—Doctrines.   I. Title.

BX1749.T6T6713 2004

230´.2—dc22

2004006128

Contents

Foreword

T HE FAME OF CERTAIN WORKS is such that it can over-
shadow their authors and the rest of their writings as
well. The *Summa theologiae* is probably the most striking
example of this. It is well known that Saint Thomas Aquinas
wrote the *Summa theologiae* and that he lived in the Middle Ages.
But few readers know what kind of man he was, the kind of life
he led, or his other writings. The renown of the title of his major
work is such that we may be surprised to learn that he wrote a
second *Summa,* the *Summa contra Gentiles,* and that several other
authors, Thomas's nearest contemporaries, also wrote their own
"Summas."

In order to understand the *Summa theologiae* better, one
should certainly become familiar with its content. But it is of
equal importance to situate it in its historical, literary, and doctrinal settings. Only in doing this can we come to appreciate its
originality. Thomas Aquinas was not like Melchisedek of the
Bible—without ancestry. He had a history that was both personal and intellectual. He drew from a number of other authors:
writers inspired by the Bible or by the ancient world; pagans and
Christians; Greek, Jewish, and Arab philosophers; theologians of
the Latin tradition that either preceded him or were contemporaneous with him; as well as eminent theologians of the Greek
and Eastern churches. Aquinas's strong personality brought unity
to all of these sources, as a great river unites its numerous tribu-

taries. Traces of these currents remain throughout his work, however, and it is important to know what they are.

The enduring quality of an author's thought is measured in part by its permanence over time and by its capacity not, as is sometimes said, to answer questions it never even asked, but to inspire solutions to problems for future generations because of the breadth of the great intuitions that govern it. Therein lies, no doubt, the major reason for the *Summa*'s lastingness and its enduring fruitfulness. The *Summa* is, of course, a work of its time, that is, of the Scholastic period, with its own tools and techniques. It is important to know how to handle and make use of them, which is not so easy at first. But once we gain a certain mastery, we come to discover the validity of the method and the richness of the content.

Sylvester of Ferrara, an enthusiastic disciple of Aquinas's, wrote of him that he was a man "for all hours." Only the future will be able to tell us whether the *Summa*, now more than seven hundred years old, is a book "for all ages." With, it must be admitted, varying degrees of success, Aquinas's disciples have strived to penetrate his thought and to bring it into dialogue with the problems of their own time. We can even marvel that his thought has been able to withstand generations of imitators. There are signs in our own day and age that show that Thomas's thought is still alive.

AQUINAS'S
Summa
Background, Structure, & Reception

The Author and His Work

S AINT AUGUSTINE'S *Confessions* are riddled with autobiographical references; the *Summa* is not as obliging about its author. It is not completely silent about him, but identifying whatever allusions there are requires supplemental information to help us understand how the personality of the man who would be its author was formed.

EARLY FORMATIVE YEARS

Thomas was born in 1224 or 1225 in the family castle of Roccasecca in southern Italy, halfway between Rome and Naples. Of the lesser nobility, his family was related to the Counts of Aquino, whence his name. As the youngest son, and according to the customs of the time, Thomas was destined for a career in the Church and became an oblate of the famous Benedictine abbey of Monte Cassino. We can only speculate about the intentions of his parents who would have liked him to become its abbot. What is certain is that it was at Monte Cassino that he received his first education. With a solid foundation in Latin letters, he acquired a deep understanding, apparent in all of his writings, of the Bible and of the writings of Gregory the Great. But above all, he acquired and maintained a contemplative orientation that was to be the distinctive mark of his theology.

In 1239, at the age of fourteen or fifteen, Thomas was sent to Naples to study at the university recently founded there by Emperor Frederick II. With the encouragement of the emperor, Sicily and southern Italy were, at this time, seats of a rich intellectual life. Because of the many translations of Michael Scotus and his school, the study of Aristotelian science, Arab astronomy, and Greek philosophy and medicine flourished at Palermo, Salerno, and Naples. Although it is difficult to be specific about what Thomas learned from two of his known teachers, Master Martin and Peter of Ireland, we know enough to understand that, very early on, he became familiar with the natural philosophy of Aristotle, the writings of the Arab commentator Averroës, and, probably, the work of the Jewish Maimonides.

It was also during this period that Thomas became acquainted with the Order of Preachers or Dominicans, who had been in Naples since 1231. In the spring of 1244, he took the habit. We can understand, even without the details of his family's opposition to this move, that his decision to enter a still young and unknown mendicant order, instead of the powerful position that his family expected of him, signaled a spiritual choice that would profoundly affect his personality and his work. This is clear in his writings on the religious life, in which he reveals his attachment to the intellectual ideal of study, teaching, and preaching, to the poverty of his mendicant order, and, especially, to his love for Christ crucified.

Thomas was sent to Paris in 1245 to continue his studies. For three years he worked under the direction of Albert the Great. I cannot emphasize enough the importance of his first stay in Paris, then the intellectual capital of Christendom. The convent of Saint Jacques where Thomas lived was the center of lively research. Under the direction of Hugh of Saint-Cher, a team of scholars had just completed work on correcting the text of the Vulgate and creating a concordance. Another team, under the direction of Vincent of Beauvais (who was still at Saint Jacques before departing to teach at Royaumont in 1246), was in the process of compiling the *Speculum maius*, a kind of encyclopedia of all the knowledge available at the time and a work that had a lasting influence. The history of this period has not been well researched, but it remains certain that Thomas found there a rich library, a fervent religious atmosphere, and favorable models for his own spiritual and intellectual development.

Under the direction of his master, for whom he performed some transcription work, Thomas pursued his theological formation and became familiar with the ethics of Aristotle and the work of Pseudo-Dionysius. He frequented the Faculty of Arts (whose philosophers were becoming more and more protective of the autonomy of their discipline) where later, because of his writings, he would have considerable influence and would leave a lasting impression even at the time of his death.

When Albert left for Cologne to found a house of studies that would later become a university, Thomas accompanied him, acting as his assistant from 1248 to 1252. It was there that he began his teaching career with a reading course on the prophet Isaiah. This work of the young scholar is one of the rare handwritten pieces we have and, if handwriting analysis sheds some light on his psychological makeup, it is also noteworthy for its marginal notes in which Thomas takes pains to point out the pastoral and spiritual implications of the biblical text. In his later writings Thomas will not call attention to this dimension so obviously, but for those who read attentively, the spiritual quality will never disappear from his theology.

Having finished his first cycle of studies in 1252, Thomas returned to Paris with the task of making a commentary on the *Sentences* of Peter Lombard. The latter, who was bishop of Paris one hundred years earlier and a teacher at the cathedral school of Notre Dame, had put together a collection of various opinions *(sententiae)* of the Fathers of the Church and of medieval theologians, grouping them together into four books according to the four major topics of sacred doctrine: the Trinity in its undivided essence and in three Persons; God the Creator and his work; the Incarnation and Redemption; the sacraments and the last things.

Because of its convenience, this general framework was quickly adopted, and Lombard's *Sentences* had become, since about 1220, the manual that each new teacher was expected to use as a basis for his teaching. And this is what Thomas did between 1252 and 1254. After his bachelor's training in the Bible at Cologne for two years, Thomas thus became a bachelor of the *Sentences,* thereby finishing the second step required for the Master's degree in Theology. This he did under the direction of Master Elijah Brunet from Bergerac. There remained one final step: that of a "formed bachelor" *[formatus]*, during which his main task would be to assist his master in public discussions and to complete the compilation of his oral commentary on Lombard's text.

This commentary was an enormous book (it would be equivalent to about 6,000 pages of modern print). Thomas expanded the original fourfold, with no fear of departing from it or eventually of contradicting it. If we were thinking above all of

Thomas's future work, we would want to underscore the novelty of this undertaking; novelty is, in fact, discernible here and there, but to insist on it would require doing a bit of apologetics. For we cannot forget that at this point Thomas, while no longer an apprentice, was still a young theologian. It is understandable, then, that he would, at least in the first book, borrow heavily from both his master Albert and from his near contemporary, the Franciscan, Bonaventure. In fact, we can already see his astonishing care to provide documentation from the frequency of Thomas's citations: Aristotle (2000), Augustine (1000), Gregory the Great (280), Dionysius the Areopagite (500), John Damascene (240), et cetera. It is important to point this out because it is a trait that will never disappear. In other words, Thomas did not think in a vacuum, but in dialogue with all of the thinkers available to him.

The final steps leading to the Master's degree took place in the spring of 1256, and Thomas was admitted into the ranks of the professors by the bishop of Paris. He thus became a "master of the biblical sciences" [*magister in sacra pagina*]. In this capacity, he was first and foremost a commentator on Sacred Scripture and a theologian who took pains to explain the doctrines of the faith. As a "master in theology" (the word "theologian" was just beginning to gain currency and does not mean exactly what we understand it to mean today), he had three fundamental tasks: *legere* "to read," that is, to comment on Scripture by means of teaching; *disputare* "to dispute," that is, to engage in a kind of teaching that involved responding to objections on a given theme; *praedicare* "to preach," that is, to explain Sacred Scripture to a broader audience. As astonishing as it may seem to us, the statutes of the University required preaching as a part of a professor's duties. As a member of the Order of Preachers, Thomas had therefore two reasons to exercise the third obligation of preaching. And he never failed to do so. About one hundred of his sermons have been preserved, three of the most important series of which are on the Lord's Prayer, the Creed, and the Ten Commandments.

As for his courses on the Bible, which were a daily obligation (at least during his tenure in Paris), several commentaries on the Old Testament have been preserved. In addition to his lectures on Isaiah, Thomas also commented on Jeremiah and Lamentations (probably before 1252, as in the case of Isaiah), the book of Job (at Orvieto, 1261–65), and a part of the book of Psalms (at Naples in 1273; death impeded him from going beyond Psalm 53). In the New Testament, he commented on the gospels according to Matthew (at Paris, 1269–70) and John (at Paris, 1270–72) and all of Saint Paul, in particular the Letter to the Romans (probably at Naples, 1272–73). As for the other letters, we cannot give precise dates.

We will examine Thomas's scriptural exegesis in more detail later but should return to the details of his life, where more remains to be said about the concrete ways in which he exercised his teaching duties. As far as we can reconstruct it with a minimum of certainty, a typical day at Saint Jacques was spent in the following way: very early in the morning Thomas gave his lecture on the Bible, which probably lasted for about two hours; after this, his assistant would lecture; in the afternoon, both of them would meet with their students to "dispute" a previously chosen topic. Because the three hours devoted to this exercise were insufficient to exhaust the topic, they proceeded by "articles," that is, by successive subdivisions that corresponded more or less to a given meeting. Eventually, certain very brief articles would be joined together into one meeting, while others that were longer or more problematical, could be split up into several sessions. The result of these discussions—comprising the difficulties or objections raised by the participants, the responses of the assistant, and the final clarification *(determinatio)* of the professor—were later put together by the professor in a completed form for the purpose of publishing it as part of a final synthesis of the question. It was thus that the development of *De veritate,* for example, disputed at Paris during Thomas's first stay there, was spread out over three years (1256–59), with eighty articles being discussed per year, roughly corresponding to the annual number of teaching days.

RETURN TO ITALY: ORVIETO (1261–1265)

At the end of the 1258–59 academic year, Thomas left Paris for Italy, probably Naples, but this is not certain. It is likely that he enjoyed a period of relative leisure, allowing him the time to make a little headway in writing the *Summa contra Gentiles,* which he had begun before leaving Paris. What is clear is that he was assigned to Orvieto in September 1261. It was there that he finished writing the *Summa contra Gentiles* and also began to write the *Exposition on Job (Expositio super Job),* two works that are among his most important. We will return to the latter, but now we must turn our attention to the *Summa contra Gentiles.*

With the *Summa theologiae,* the *Summa contra Gentiles* (sometimes called simply the *Contra Gentiles)* is, without a doubt, the best known of Thomas Aquinas's works. As to the structure of the work and its audience, a range of opinions has been proposed, too broad to debate here, but there is one that we can definitely exclude: the *Summa contra Gentiles* is not a "Summa" of philosophy. It is, rather, a theological project, as its recourse to arguments from authority (Scripture, the Church Fathers, and the Creeds) amply shows.

This work, divided into four parts, has as its aim to study all that human reason can know about God. First, what is proper to God in himself, his existence and his perfection (Book I). Then, the going out of creatures from God, that is, the creative act itself and its effects (Book II). Third, the orientation of creatures to God as to their end, what Thomas calls the divine government (Book III). It is important to keep this outline in mind. Not only does it sketch out the plan for the first three books, but it also recalls what Thomas strove to find in the *Sentences* of Lombard, and it clearly prefigures the circular plan that he will follow in the *Summa theologiae:* everything comes from God and everything returns to him under his guidance. As for Book IV, Thomas deals with truths that are completely inaccessible to human reason and are known only by revelation: the Trinitarian dimension of God, the incarnation of the Word and his work of salvation, the sacraments, and the final end of the human person.

This brief presentation would be inexact if I failed to mention that which gives the *Contra Gentiles* its particular character. Thomas is not some disinterested sage "explaining the truth professed by the Catholic faith and rejecting contrary errors." Rather, his commitment to the truth is so personal that his statement of intent in writing the *Contra Gentiles* contains the surprising statement: "my principal aim in life, to which I feel obligated in conscience before God, is that all of my words and sentiments speak of him" (I.9). Often cited as one of those rare passages in which Thomas allows a glimpse of himself, this statement is a good indication of the value of the *Summa contra Gentiles*. R.-A. Gauthier, one of this work's finest scholars, expresses it best when he writes that "Thomas made being a theologian his life. This is the secret of his work."

We will not find this kind of intimate detail in the *Summa theologiae*, even though it was a project dear to Thomas. How personal it was can be appreciated if we understand why Thomas was sent to Orvieto in the first place. It is important to note that for a variety of reasons most Dominicans (nine out of ten) could not study in the universities and so had to content themselves with a much more modest formation. For these Dominicans, the Order had put in place a system of what we would call today "continuing education" given by one of their members in order to arm his confreres better for their two primary missions: preaching and hearing confessions. It was precisely this role that Thomas was to fulfill.

Among the tools at his disposal was a series of moral manuals. While useful, these manuals also had their weaknesses: different virtues or different sins or even different sacraments were treated one after the other in order to examine the concrete problems that they posed. What one does not find in them, however, is a concern to establish Christian morality on Gospel foundations or to connect the various parts into a unified whole. Moreover, the properly dogmatic formation in the great truths of the faith was dangerously neglected. If it is the case that the teaching he was doing allowed Thomas to establish the foundations of what he would discuss later in the moral part of the *Summa,* it is also likely that he was aware of the partial and deficient formation received by his young confreres. It was probably because of this that he conceived the idea of a new work that would treat of the whole of theology, both dogmatic and moral, in a comprehensive and organically structured way. The *Summa theologiae* thus had its beginnings in Thomas's pedagogical concerns.

STAY IN ROME (1265–1268)

Solid arguments can be given in support of this thesis. In fact, as soon as Thomas had finished writing what he had already begun, he started drafting his new work (that is, the *Summa theologiae*). In the meantime, he changed residences and, in 1265, found himself in Rome, where he was charged with establishing a special house of studies over which he would have complete authority, including in regard to the choice of students, the subjects taught, and the method of teaching. Little evidence remains regarding the concrete development of this experiment, but we are pretty well informed concerning what Thomas was writing at this time.

In addition to the First Part of the *Summa,* Thomas also completed another book, which he had begun at Orvieto at the request of Pope Urban IV: the *Golden Chain (Catena aurea).* This verse-by-verse commentary on the four Gospels, using a series of extracts from the Fathers of the Church, is arranged in such a way as to allow for a continuous reading. The speed with which he wrote this work (four volumes spread out between 1263 and 1268) suggests that Thomas had the help of several persons working as a team under his direction. They gathered the texts according to his instructions and he reserved to himself the finishing touches. What could have been nothing more than a massive compilation is, in reality, a well-constructed work, one which plays an important role in the subsequent work of

Thomas and which will have considerable influence in the history of theology.

During his stay in Rome, Thomas also wrote the disputed questions *On the Power of God (De potentia Dei)*, a lengthy work comparable, if not in size then at least in depth, to the questions *On Truth (De veritate)*. At the same time, he also wrote the first part of the *Compendium theologiae* and, as he had already done at Orvieto, several other works in response to various requests. It should be noted that sacred science, as the summit of knowledge, required that the master be not only versed in philosophy, but also competent in all other sciences as well. While I cannot go into detail about this here, I should mention that Thomas wrote twenty-six small works at the request of disciples and friends, the Master of the Dominican order, the Pope, and even different princes, thus demonstrating that he was very much involved in the events of the time and attentive to the concerns of his contemporaries. To cite but a few examples: Thomas wrote about the movements of the heart, the hidden forces of nature, the influence of stars on human life, wizardry, commercial fraud, business ethics (the charging of interest, buying on credit, speculation), the legality of taxes, and so forth.

But this period is especially significant for the fact that, in addition to the *Summa,* Thomas began a new project that would occupy him for the rest of his life. At the end of his stay in Rome, 1267–68, he began work on *On the Soul,* which inaugurated a series of twelve commentaries on Aristotle. He did not complete all of them but some he did, including, in addition to *On the Soul,* the *Nicomachean Ethics,* the *Physics,* the *Metaphysics,* the *Peri Hermeneias* and the *Posterior Analytics,* some of them quite lengthy. Granted what we know from other sources, namely, that these commentaries were not presented orally, a question then arises: what impelled Thomas, already overworked, to launch this new enterprise?

We can answer this question in two ways. First of all, this is how Thomas prepared for his own books. While familiarizing himself with the thought of the Greek philosopher, he would discover the different aspects of a subject, and could thus treat of it with greater mastery. The commentary on *On the Soul* was written in tandem with the end of the First Part of the *Summa* where Thomas discusses his anthropology. In the same way, his study of the *Nicomachean Ethics* is contemporaneous with his writing of the Second Part of the *Summa*. Elsewhere, we see Thomas simultaneously writing the third book of the *Contra Gentiles* and his *Exposition on Job,* both of which treat of the question of Providence. This way of proceeding is thus frequent.

The second reason is more apostolic. His commentaries were not the subject of oral teaching. Nonetheless they were distributed and read, first by his colleagues who, perhaps, encouraged him to write them, then by others who knew of their existence. Thomas's intention was not as gratuitous as we might imagine; his aim was not simply to research and share what Aristotle thought. As he repeated many times, the interest for him of the ancients lay less in what they thought than in seeking the truth with them. By explaining Aristotle through Christian lenses, he was able, at the same time, to strip Aristotle of his paganism, thus fulfilling the intellectual apostolate which he saw not only as the mission of his order, but as his own personal mission.

RETURN TO PARIS (1268–1272)

Three reasons seem to have played a role in Thomas's being sent back to Paris by his superiors. At the faculty of Theology he had to confront the extreme conservatives who saw in Aristotle a danger to the Christian faith. On the opposite front, he had to deal with what would later be called monopsychism: the belief, based on Averroës, that there was only one thinking intellect for all of humanity. Lastly, he also had to defend the mendicant orders against the secular masters who wished to exclude them from university teaching.

Regarding the first of these three reasons: all of Thomas's work argues for the full recognition of the rights of nature and of reason even with respect to the faith. But the discussion centered on two burning questions: the eternity of the world, to which Thomas devoted a short work by the same name; and the unicity of the soul within the human being, about which he speaks each time he deals with anthropology. The second question gave birth to one of his most famous works, *On the Unity of the Intellect against Averroës* which, even today, is highly esteemed by philosophers. As for the dispute with the secular masters, this was but an acute phase of their tenacious opposition to the mendicants. The Franciscans were also implicated in this opposition and Saint Bonaventure sided with Thomas. This hostility would last beyond the lives of these two men, but we owe to this dispute three wonderful little books on the idea of religious life as Thomas saw it, especially that of the Dominicans. In reading them, we also discover a scathing polemicist, which does not all fit the conventional image we have of him.

What is more illuminating from a historical perspective is

that these three activities did not have exclusive claim on Thomas's time. Quite the contrary: the daily life of the university continued to make its demands and we now enjoy its fruits. It was during this time that Thomas wrote his commentaries on both Matthew and John, on certain disputed questions such as *On Evil (De malo),* as well as other more modest works such as the *Quodlibets.* These disputed questions, which each master had to present publicly twice a year (at Christmas and Easter) and during which he had to respond to questions, were risky exercises. Not only did he face unexpected questions but vindictive colleagues as well, who used these occasions to trap him. Many even tried to shirk this obligation, but not so Thomas.

While all of this activity was going on, Thomas was also writing opuscules in response to those who consulted him, as well as continuing his work on the commentaries of Aristotle. But this was especially a period in which he worked on the *Summa.* Although the First Part was completed before he left Rome, it was not until the final months of 1270 that Thomas was able to resume work on it. He worked with such intensity that he completed the enormous Second Part (303 questions treated in some two thousand pages) in eighteen months.

The abundance of his literary output is hard to believe. But the facts are there. Each day during this period, Thomas would write the equivalent of twelve pages of small type. Such a production cannot be explained by the work of one person alone. Like his predecessors, Hugh of Saint-Cher and Vincent of Beauvais, Thomas had a team of secretaries at his disposal (we know the names of some of them). They prepared the work and wrote it down while Thomas, more often than not, *dictated.* There was often not enough time during the working day to finish the task at hand. This suggests, as the evidence shows, that Thomas was in the habit of spending a good part of his nights at work.

NAPLES: THE LAST MONTHS AND DEATH (1272–1274)

It was thus an already tired man who left for Naples in the spring of 1272. His superiors sent him to the city of his youth to establish a new house of studies that would become the Faculty of Theology of the university. From what we know of the man Thomas, this was a privileged time. We see him renewing contact with his family, his sisters and nieces, and many others who, still alive thirty-five years later, would testify at his process of canonization.

To continue with our intellectual biography: Thomas's role of professor continued during the following year, 1272–73 (from September to the end of November 1273). In public, he gave a course on the Epistle to the Romans and the Psalms; in private, he continued his commentary on Aristotle and his writing of the *Summa*. Certain scholars believe that Thomas had already written the first questions of the Third Part of the *Summa* before leaving Paris. But the trip, the new foundation, and other circumstances (e.g., he was the executor of the estate of his brother-in-law, Roger of Aquila) no doubt cost him a lot of time. Thus, when he was obliged to stop working, he had made little progress on his great work. He did manage to finish the part on Christ, but only began the part on the sacraments (Baptism, the Eucharist, and Penance).

At around the Feast of Saint Nicholas, December 6, 1273, Thomas stopped teaching and writing completely. To Raynald, his assistant and friend, who did not understand why he had abandoned his work, Thomas's only response was: "I cannot.

Everything I have written seems like so much straw in comparison to what I have seen." He was sent to his sister's, in the vicinity of Naples, to rest. But his silence continued. Shortly thereafter he was on the road again in response to Pope Gregory X's call that he come to Lyons to help prepare the upcoming council. While on the way, he hit his head against a tree. It seemed only a light wound, but several days later he had to take to his bed. He died on March 7, 1274, at the Cistercian abbey of Fossanova. He was not yet fifty years old.

Historians have speculated much about what might have happened during these last months. It is possible that overwork might have caused a physical and nervous breakdown. But we cannot disregard a series of mystical experiences, mentioned by biographers, that might have led to his desire to leave this life. The accident on the road was no doubt the proximate cause of death, but Thomas remained fully in control of his intellectual faculties. His *Letter to the Abbot of Monte Cassino,* written after this event, is his most luminous explanation of the relationship between the infallibility of the divine foreknowledge and human freedom.

Already controversial while living, Thomas was even more so after his death. His canonization in 1323 gave him personally some protection. But although he had faithful disciples, his teaching continued to incite opposition, and his being named a Doctor of the Church by Pius V in 1567 did nothing to change that. The opinion to the contrary is but a recent error of perspective. There is no small paradox in the fact that one who became known as the "common" Doctor *[doctor communis]* was so little that. In truth, he was not "common" in either of the two meanings of this word.

The *Summa*

Structures and Content I

P EOPLE HAVE OFTEN compared the structure of the medieval *Summas* of theology to that of the medieval
cathedrals. This image is a cliché and says nothing as
long as we do not understand how this architecture was laid out.
This is the first thing that we have to look at. For the sake of argument, let us suppose a reader with no idea how this book is
laid out. My description would go from the exterior to the interior and from the more material to the more formal. This is the
preferred method of Thomas himself who recommends that one
proceed from the more known to the less known.

Certain editions of the *Summa* are printed on bible paper in
one volume; this is the exception. These have the advantage of
underscoring the organic unity of the work: it is one book that
speaks of one and the same subject. Other editions can have as
many as sixty-eight volumes. This expansion, owing to the notes
and commentaries that accompany the text, is also exceptional.
The usefulness of these editions is to emphasize that this one
work contains a number of individual treatises. Between these
two extremes, the usual way in which the *Summa* has been presented since it left its author's hands is in four volumes, and this

structure divides the work into parts that he wished to be artic-
ulated.

Still, this material presentation in four volumes is not without problems for, in reality, a tripartite plan structures the whole.
Thomas is clear on this: he will speak first of God (I), then of the
movement of the rational creature to God (II), and finally, of
Christ who, in his humanity, is the way that leads to God (III).
The great simplicity of this outline is not very explicit and it,
too, is not without problems. But things will become clearer little by little. Before leaving behind this elementary approach to
the text, I should add that the move from three parts to four volumes is the result of the division of the Second Part into two—
for practical reasons (a question of length) but also because of
the nature of the material itself.

The First Part

The first volume can be identified with the First Part (we usually refer to it as the *Prima Pars* or simply the *Prima* or shortened
to Ia; this will be the same for the other parts). The First Part begins with a general Prologue in which Thomas explains what he
will do. While often cited, these few lines are not always well understood:

Since the doctor of the Catholic truth must not only teach the most ad-
vanced but also instruct beginners . . . my intention is to explain what
concerns the Christian religion in a way that is appropriate for the formation of beginners.

We can ask ourselves: what were the intellectual gifts of these
"beginners" to whom Thomas offered a work of such quality? It
is not impossible that he overestimated the capacities of his read-

ers. But no doubt he was thinking less about the level of difficulty of the material taught than about its organization into a body of doctrine that would offer them not simply a series of questions juxtaposed haphazardly, but rather an organic synthesis in which the internal connections and coherence of these questions might be grasped. He writes:

> We have seen in fact that, in the use of the writings of different authors, novices are a little uneasy, either because of the multiplication of useless questions, articles, and proofs, or because what they need to learn is not treated according to the requirements of the material taught [*secundum ordinem disciplinae*] but instead according to what the explanation of books or the occasion of debates requires. Lastly, the frequent repetition of the same things can produce, in the minds of the listeners, both lassitude and confusion. Desirous of avoiding these shortcomings, I will attempt, with the divine aid, to present sacred doctrine in as clear and brief a manner as the material permits.

These are the concerns and the intentions of a teacher, and they can be understood better in the context of his experiences at Orvieto. In all likelihood, it is probably more difficult for us to read the *Summa* than it was for Thomas's contemporaries. But if we are attentive to the directions he gives us, we will be able to benefit from it as well.

"SACRA DOCTRINA"

The first question is a kind of discourse on method. In it, the author presents his understanding of "sacred doctrine" [*sacra doctrina*], which encompasses our current understanding of "theology" and goes beyond it, since the term includes all forms of Christian teaching, beginning with what God says to us in Sacred Scripture. Following the usage of his time, he asks himself if it confirms the Aristotelian concept of "science," that is, if it is able, among other things, to advance the reasoned knowledge that we have of God by placing in relation the diverse truths that we believe. In accordance with this ideal of knowledge, and since science is a knowledge through causes, it can be said of two given truths that one can play the role of an explanatory cause and the other that of the effect explained.

We will see examples of this later on. But if one does not want to be entirely mistaken, it is best to clarify two things about this particular kind of knowledge right away. First, sacred doctrine is not really "science" because of its total subordination by faith to the knowledge that it receives from God (Thomas speaks here of "subalternation"). Outside of this relationship of dependence to faith, which establishes that about which it speaks and gives to it both its relevance and love, not only would theology have no justification, but it would literally have no object. Second, more than "science," which is merely knowledge by proximate causes, sacred doctrine is "wisdom," that is, knowledge by the supreme cause. Seen from this perspective, the reciprocal relationships between the truths of the faith are organized into a body of knowledge that has God as its keystone. We can sense immediately the strength and intention of this approach: God presents himself as the first subject of theology, and it is with respect to him that all of the rest is situated, not in the sense of being juxtaposed to him, but rather dependent on him and explained by him. For, coming from him and returning to him:

All things in *sacra doctrina* are considered from the point of view of God. It is either about God himself, or about things in the measure in which they have God as their source and their end. It follows that God is truly the subject of this science (Ia q. 1, a 7).

GOD

After the introductory question, the first volume is divided into three clearly distinct sections: God considered from the point of view of the divine essence; God from the point of view of the distinction of persons; the way in which creatures proceed from God. Before going into detail, we should note that one frequently hears the first section (qq. 2–26) referred to as "Saint Thomas's treatise on God" and it has often been used to create a theodicy, a *philosophical* treatise on God. This is not in keeping with the intentions of the author. He is writing a Summa of *theology* and the God about whom he speaks has nothing in common with that spoken of by the deist philosophers but is instead the living God of the Bible, who has revealed himself in salvation history. Knowledge of him is not attained until he has been understood as a trinity of persons. This is why the *Summa*'s treatise on God ends with the question of the plurality of Persons in the Trinity, what distinguishes them and what is proper to each of them. The break between the two sections serves only a pedagogical function; it should not be understood as a separation.

Thomas, if we follow him, explains the way in which he has divided his first section: "It has to be asked first *if God exists;* then, what is the manner of his existence, or better yet what is not the manner of his existence; finally, we must investigate his operations: his knowledge, his will, and his power."

When Thomas asks himself about the existence of God (q. 2), it is not because he doubts it. Contrary to what we might think at first, his reasoning is less directed against atheism than it is against another current of thought (ontologism), which held that the existence of God is evident and need not be established. To the advocates of this position Thomas replies: it is evident *in itself,* but not *for us.* It is in this context that he proposes five ways to establish the existence of God from created experience. These famous proofs have challenged the sagacity of generations of interpreters to whom I can only refer the reader.

Since he is speaking about God, Thomas asks himself *"what is the manner of his existence,"* or, rather *"what is not the manner of his existence"* (qq. 3–13). I call the reader's attention to the precision he brings to this question for, during the rationalist period of theology, it was somewhat misunderstood. Thomas certainly claims to be saying something about God, otherwise he would not have raised the question in the first place. But he is careful to do so with the most profound respect for the divine mystery, without thinking or letting others think that he is able to say all that can be said about him. He constantly repeats as a leitmotif: concerning God we cannot know "what he is" [*quid est*], but only "what he is not" [*quid non est*]. Without shying away from the task, for he sees the fact that intelligence is able to confront such a challenge as a proof of magnanimity, he nonetheless does not hesitate to affirm that God is "known as unknown." And if he dares to say something at all, it will be "as one stuttering." It is this backdrop that provides the setting for the following series of questions on the simplicity of God, his perfection and his goodness, his infinity and his presence in all things, his immutability and his eternity, his unity, and finally the way in which he is known by us. We cannot go into detail about all of these questions, but if a non-specialist is surprised at the slimness of the results obtained by this highly sophisticated negative dialectic, Thomas would no doubt respond that it is no mean thing to know about God what he is not.

Concerning the operation of God (qq. 14–26), Thomas begins with his knowledge and the way in which God knows things. It is here that we find the celebrated question of the divine ideas, a Christian transposition of the Ideas of Plato, following St. Augustine. But Thomas also uses this opportunity to talk about truth and the transcendentals. After examining God's existence, Thomas returns to the question of his will and, more precisely, of his love, his justice and mercy, his providence, his power, and, lastly, his beatitude. This last question may be surprising at first, but it is fairly typical of the scientific process in theology. It is not sufficient to affirm that God is the first and the supreme possessor of beatitude. Theology wants to know *why* this is so. Condensing a lot of information, we can say that God, knowing himself perfectly as supreme Being and Truth, and loving himself as the Good in itself and the source of all other goodness, cannot but be perfectly happy.

The treatise on the Trinity takes up the next sixteen questions (qq. 27–43). These questions are themselves divided into three subsections: the Persons in general, in which notably Thomas proposes his definition of person; the Persons in particular, in which he takes up again and organizes everything that can possibly be said of each of the divine Persons in a cleverly graduated order (one question for the Father, two for the Son, three for the Holy Spirit); the Persons in their mutual relationships.

This treatise on the Trinity, in which Thomas is very attentive to Scripture and the Fathers, is a masterpiece of speculative theology and it was to have a profound impact on Western theology after him. If we were to retain only a single thing from his method, it would be the force with which Thomas underscores that, under the guise of rationality, we cannot claim to prove that there must necessarily be persons in God. This is a matter of faith:

> To use reasons that are not necessary as proofs of the faith is to open the faith up to the derision of unbelievers, because they will believe that it is on the basis of these reasons that we believe. Let us not try to prove the truths of the faith other than by arguments from authority (borrowed from Scripture whose authority is revelation itself) for those who accept them. As for the others, it is enough to defend the non-impossibility of the mysteries set forth by the faith (q. 32, a. 1).

GOD IN HIS WORK

In the third section, Thomas continues to speak about God, but here he considers him in his work, of which he is and remains the Creator and "Governor." This section is also divided into three sub-sections. First, creation as an act of God, that is, the way in which creatures proceed from the Trinity. Far from showing creation as a necessity that is imposed on God, as with emanationism, Thomas, who follows the Bible, sees in it an act of wisdom and of free will, stemming from a gratuitous love that desires only to share its own good. In line with contemporary discussions of the possible eternity of the world, Thomas takes pains to disassociate the very idea of creation from that of the beginning of the world in time. Our faith confesses that the world had a beginning, but even if the world were eternal, it would be no less created since creation is the "relation of dependence of the created being with respect to its origin." One should not imagine creation as an isolated act that occurred in a distant past; rather, it is a present reality (qq. 44–46).

After these preliminary clarifications, Thomas turns his attention to creatures themselves, and first, to the "distinctions" between them, that is, to the main categories of beings that make up the created universe (qq. 47–102). A sort of introduction in three questions sets up the very notion of distinction and, more precisely, the distinction between good and evil. The essential question before all others is to account for the way in which the existence of evil can be reconciled with the universal presence and action of a supremely good creator God (qq. 47–49). In keeping with the three main categories of created beings, we find three new subdivisions: first, purely spiritual creatures called angels, whose nature and operation, both intellectual and voluntary, he examines (qq. 50–64); then, all other creatures, presented under the form of a commentary on the biblical story of creation, a classic treatise traditionally known as "the work of six days" (qq. 65–74); finally, man who, as a spiritual and corporeal creature, is made up of matter and spirit, that is, of the first two categories and who, because of this, constitutes a veritable "universe in miniature," a microcosm. Conscious of the limits of his inquiry, Thomas leaves the care of discussing the body to experimental science, restricting himself to a discussion of the intellectual and voluntary operations of the soul. It is here that we find Thomas's rational psychology, especially his theory of knowledge by abstraction from sense perceptions, of the knowledge of the soul by itself, of free will, and of the relationship between intelligence and will (qq. 75–89). Those things concerning the study of affective psychology are reserved for the Second Part, but one must never forget these important questions, questions that will constantly be presupposed in the theory of human acts that comes into play later in the *Summa*. Any anthropology claiming to take its inspiration from Master Thomas should absolutely take into account these two developments.

Thomas spends a fair amount of time on what the consequences are for man who has been created directly by God in
his image and is called to resemble him more and more each day
(qq. 90–102, see especially q. 93). Here, two things must be
stressed. First, concerning the doctrine itself, it must be said first
of all that Thomas does not consider the image of God in man
to be a static reality. Certainly there is the structural order of nature, but things play out more decisively on the order of grace,
and our resemblance will not be complete except in the beatific
vision, in which the person will know and love his Exemplar,
just as he is known and loved by him (see 1 Cor 13.12; 1 Jn 3.2).
Second, it should be underscored that recent research, which is
much more sensitive to this theme, has drawn attention to the
architectonic role that these questions play in the construction
of the *Summa:* it is around the notion of the "image of God"
that the First and Second Parts are joined together.

The First Part ends with a study of the "divine governance"
(qq. 103–19), that is, the way in which God preserves his creation
in existence and leads it to its end, by himself directly, but also by
means of secondary causes, according to the plan of his providence. A final distinction of capital importance for understanding the intention of the author is this: however much Thomas
insists on the total dependence of the creature on God, he also
insists on the consistency and autonomy of the creature once
created. Far from substituting himself for the beings that he has
called into existence, God gives them the means to move themselves and to act of their own accord, either by the laws of their
nature in the case of sub-rational creatures, or, in the case of hu-
mans, by an intelligent and free will.

This First Part of the *Summa* is a speculative construction of
the highest level, but it risks appearing a little abstract for today's

reader. It would be wrong, however, to be discouraged by its difficulty. For the person who is sufficiently motivated and who approaches the text in stages, a thorough perusal is not only fruitful, it is decisive for understanding man's situation in this world. In perfect harmony with what revelation tells us about this situation, Thomas Aquinas proposes a view of man and of the created universe that fully respects the reality of their autonomy and greatness. He has no difficulty recognizing the supreme nobility and dignity of the human person in nature, for—as he enjoys repeating—even grace needs nature. Grace must bring nature to its perfection, not destroy it.

The Second Part

As I have said, two volumes were required for the Second Part. Those who are familiar with Master Thomas speak of the *Prima Secundae* (literally: the first of the second! or Ia IIae) and of the *Secunda Secundae* (IIa IIae). The reason for this division is easy to understand as soon as one realizes its incredible dimensions. It has 1,535 articles assembled into 303 questions. The details of its construction will have to wait, but for now it is important to grasp the overarching unity of the design of the whole.

A CIRCULAR PLAN

At the very beginning, Thomas tells us that he wants to speak of God as the source and end of all creatures. This fundamental fact, which governs the entire organization of the *Summa,* is like a subterranean current that unifies, by tying together, the three parts and their multiple treatises. There is a structure underlying this multiplicity: the work is in fact constructed according to a circular plan that draws the reader into the "going-out-from-returning-to" [*exitus-reditus*] movement which is that of the entire universe, coming from God its creator and returning to him as its final end. Thomas may have borrowed this notion from the Neoplatonism of his masters, but he had long been familiar with the idea. It was already found in the Bible where God is referred to as the Alpha and Omega of all things. The practical value of this insight becomes eminently clear in the Second Part since man, as a free person, has the privilege of consciously embracing this movement:

Man, being made in the image of God—by which, according to John Damascene, we must understand that he is endowed with intelligence, free will, and the power of autonomous action—we must now, after having spoken of the Exemplar . . . take up that which concerns his image, which is to say man, insofar as *he too* is the source of his own acts by virtue of his free will and the mastery of his actions (Ia IIae, Prol.).

The major points of this short text are clear enough. The mention of the Exemplar and the image refers unmistakably to the end of the First Part where man is presented as the image of God. Here moreover, Thomas underscores that this partner that God gives himself is, "he too," the master of his actions in his own way. By doing so, Thomas brings to the fore the connection between the First and Second Parts and the greatness of him whom God calls to share his life. As an introduction to this new part that he is beginning, we find the following at the start of the first question:

First of all, we must consider the final end of human life, then ask by what means man attains it or turns away from it. For it is according the *end* that we gain an idea of the *means* (literally: of that which is related to it).

It is both instructive and startling at the same time to see that the complexity and enormity of this Second Part, with its innumerable refined and detailed reflections, are summarized into two essential categories: the *ends* and the *means*. Five questions will suffice to discuss the end. But the category of the "means" is so vast that it takes up the rest of the second and third volumes. Thomas will return to it again under another aspect in the Third Part.

The most important thing to keep in mind, and I cannot insist on this enough, is this: if we want to grasp Thomas's plan and his originality, we have to appreciate the fact that he situates human action in its totality between two considerations of the ultimate end: at its origin—for in the order of aim or intention, the end is first (in other words, one has to know and love the end in order to be directed to it)—but also at its completion, for in the order of concrete execution, the end is the last thing achieved. Moreover, the end will not effectively be achieved without grace and without following Christ who came to show us, in his humanity, the way to happiness. This was the first word of the *Summa,* but Thomas has no fear of repeating himself here. Between the study of human action described in the Second Part and that of the happy life which concludes the *Summa,* Thomas will insert, in the Third Part, a study of Christ—"the unique mediator between God and humanity" (1 Tim 2.5)—and of the sacraments which are part of the "means" left to his followers to assist them in reaching their end. We will look at the content of this last part later, but it should be said now that the study of the *reditus,* that is, of the return of man to God, is not completed at the end of the Second Part. Thomas will pursue it again in the *Tertia* because this return is not brought to completion except by Christ and in him.

THE SECOND VOLUME

The second volume thus corresponds to the *Prima Secundae.* It begins, as I have just said, with a consideration of beatitude (Ia IIae qq. 1–5). Short in length, precise in subject matter, this opening treatise is characteristic of the construction of the *Summa.* In placing it in the opening position, Thomas differs from his contemporaries who place it last. If it seems like he is agreeing with Aristotle—who also speaks of happiness in the first and last books of the *Ethics*—he quickly parts from him with the definition that he gives of happiness. At the end of an argument in which he eliminates in turn all that is not happiness (wealth, honors, glory, power, health, and pleasures), Thomas arrives at the ultimate end that is actually being sought through and beyond all of these transitory goods: God himself. Thus the notion of some kind of a vague happiness more or less consciously pursued, gives place to a clearly identified happiness that can only lie in the loving contemplation of God, the sole object of happiness.

Thomas's choice, so characteristic of his way of proceeding, to place the discussion of beatitude at the beginning and at the end implies a singular way of envisaging human action and its motivations. His moral theology is not expressed, as most are, in terms of obligation, but in terms of the search for happiness. Far from being structured around the imperative to obey an exterior law, it knows no other law but the law of love. Master Thomas would even go so far as to say that an act done merely out of obedience to the law lacks something essential to virtue, namely, that the person be moved to the good by himself and not by constraint. His is a morality of freedom; it is entirely oriented toward fulfilling the Gospel in oneself.

This general perspective allows us to understand better the internal aim and organization of the Second Part. Since it deals with "human acts in order to know which ones lead us to happiness and which ones prevent our attaining it" (Ia IIae q. 6, Prol.), the manner of consideration must proceed in two registers. First, given that human acts are the object of a science, they must be considered *in general* (in the *Prima Secundae*). Second, because that science is a *practical* science, from which no conclusions can be drawn except by looking at each particular concrete act, the moral consideration focuses its study on providing direction to action (this will be in the *Secunda Secundae*). Nevertheless, even in the *Secunda Secundae,* Thomas does not allow himself to stoop to the pratico-practical level of the casuists (which was precisely the weakness of the manuals he once used at Orvieto). He always remains at the level of a kind of knowledge that we can qualify as speculatively practical: practical because directed to a certain end; speculative because it confines itself to a reflective level without trying to dictate every last prescription. These final applications of practical reason require the prior presence of the virtue of prudence.

HUMAN ACTS

Now that we have understood these essential points, it is possible to cover quickly the different treatises and to grasp their arrangement within the *Prima Secundae*. Immediately following his study of beatitude, Thomas takes up the question of human acts (qq. 6–89). He first looks at them insofar as they are formally human, that is, as voluntary and free, for it is only under this aspect that they can be good or bad. It is true that the object, the circumstances, and especially the end enter into an appreciation of human acts, but these are called moral solely in an analogous sense. Only a human act that is sufficiently free and conscious is formally the subject of morality, and only to the extent that it conforms to reason made right by the Gospel is it morally good.

Man, however, because he is a body-soul unity, is not simply made up of two spiritual faculties of the soul, intelligence and will, which are principally determinative. We must also consider his sense knowledge and his sense appetites, in other words, the affective factors that also play a role in the quality of his actions. As a seasoned moralist, Thomas gives a large place to all that comes from the sensitive appetite, what he calls the "passions" of the soul. He will also treat of these in a new and original way. In and of themselves, the passions thus understood are neither good nor bad. It is because of the unity of the human composite that they become voluntary by participation and, as such, can be morally good or bad according as they are subject or not to the superior faculties, which, in turn, are enlightened by the Gospel (qq. 22–48).

Having mastered these general notions, we can now turn our attention to the *interior principles* that qualify the soul's powers regarding action. These are called *habitus* (from the Latin *habeo,* i.e., "to have"). We should be cautious about translating this word as our word "habit" for it does not mean the same thing at all. In fact, it means the contrary. While a habit is a fixed mechanism, a routine, a *habitus* is, on the contrary, an inventive capacity, perfective of the faculty in which it is found and to which it gives perfect freedom in its exercise. At the midpoint between a nature and its action, the *habitus* is the sign and expression of its full flourishing (qq. 49–54). This is so at least for the *virtuous habitus,* which perfect the person in the direction of his nature, oriented toward the good, thus leading him to happiness.

In the first presentation of the virtues that we read in the *Prima Secundae*, we find first of all an explanation of the differences between the intellectual and the moral virtues, the cardinal virtues and the theological virtues (qq. 55–67). We will find the same discussion in the *Secunda Secundae*, but before we get to that, Thomas places here, in the *Prima Secundae*, a beautiful little treatise on the fruits of the Holy Spirit and their accompanying joys. This is a way of calling our attention to the fact that the happiness that comes from acting, even virtuous acting, cannot be realized on a purely human level. The Holy Spirit, the interior master, must intervene at the very depth of the human heart to enlighten it and to move it in the direction of the true good (qq. 68–70). However, and this is also part of what it means to be human, there are also bad *habitus,* the vices or sins that, while developing the perfective ease that is implied in the notion of *habitus,* are exercised in a direction that turns away from the final end and so lead us astray (qq. 71–89). A substantial treatise is devoted to them, so we know what we are dealing with. But it must also be said that its place in the movement of the whole does not emphasize sin. Thomas's attention is positively oriented.

LAW AND GRACE

Thomas sees other principles at work in the human act, but this time they are *exterior* to the person. He distinguishes two, one of them being Satan, who pushes man toward evil through temptation. But since he has already talked about this elsewhere (Ia q. 114), he does not come back to it here. There is of course another external principle, which makes us act well, God himself, who instructs man by the law. What we have said concerning the inherent freedom of human action is not contradicted in the least by the high esteem in which Thomas holds the law. Dependent on the eternal law, which is itself identified with the divine government, that is, with Providence, the natural law is the participation of the eternal law in the rational creature. It is natural law that finds expression in various kinds of positive law in such a way that man, by following the prescriptions of the law, is called to be his own providence: "God left man to his own counsel" (Sir 15.14). With this biblical phrase, Thomas reconciles both law and freedom (qq. 90–97). But God has reserved himself the right to intervene in salvation history. Thus, he promulgated two kinds of law: the *Old Law,* which Thomas examines in minute detail (qq. 98–105), and the *New Law,* which Thomas identifies with the grace of the Holy Spirit (qq. 106–8).

The whole of this treatise with its three subdivisions deserves to be known better. It is a magnificent apologia for the law. While Thomas highlights the great educative value of the law for personal freedom and stresses its necessary role in service to the common good, he also radically relativizes it, since its usefulness is only pedagogical and disappears once its service is completed.

God is not content with instructing us from the exterior by the law. He also supports us by his grace. This "external" transcendent principle is at the origin of the powers and of the *habitus* that perfect the creature from the *interior* and allow him to act on another plane, one superior to the one he received by nature at birth, that of the divine life given at baptism (qq. 109–14). This treatise on grace is noteworthy in the overall structure of the *Summa.* Thomas is neither the first nor the only to speak of grace, but he is unique in the way that he does so. Contrary to Peter Lombard, who identifies the love in our hearts with the

Holy Spirit himself who moves our free will to love and to act well, Thomas insists that we have to distinguish between the source of love, which is indeed the Holy Spirit, and the love which is in us, which is necessarily a created gift. Otherwise, it would not be us acting but rather the Holy Spirit in us. But if grace takes the form of a created *habitus,* then it is we, cooperating with the Holy Spirit, who are the authors of our own acts. This free and graced activity will even be our way of working for our happiness in the heavenly homeland.

It is profoundly significant that the treatise on grace comes at the end of the *Prima Secundae,* and it is easy to understand the reason. This volume begins with the final end that man pursues in all his actions, and everything that follows is an examination of the means that allow him to attain this end. The a priori condition that has been assumed but until now not examined, is that an act must be proportionate to the end that one wishes to attain. Now since this end is beatitude—the enjoyment of God in a perfect communion of knowledge and love—it is completely disproportionate to human capabilities. By definition, this kind of happiness is connatural only to God. God, therefore, must provide man not only with the wherewithal to act in view of this end and to have his desire inclined to it, but also with the means by which human nature itself can be raised to the heights of that end. This is what the created gift of grace responds to, and with this Thomas concludes the *Prima Secundae:* God "equips" man in such a way as to allow him to attain by his free and virtuous acts the end to which he calls him.

What follows in the Second Part examines these acts in detail. However, before moving on, we should take note of a feaure of Thomas's procedure that might strike us as peculiar. We expect to find distinctions in the *Summa* between exegesis and theology, or again between speculative theology and pragmatic theology, or yet between dogmatic and moral theology. We have the tendency to identify dogmatic theology with the First and Third Parts (God and Christ) and moral theology with the Second Part. But this does not correspond at all with what Saint Thomas does. The Second Part is certainly dominated by moral questions, but the treatises on grace, the theological virtues, and original sin are without doubt dogmatic questions. In the same way, the anthropological questions of the *Prima Pars* deal more with moral issues than with dogmatic ones strictly speaking. Moreover, Thomas uses scriptural and patristic references constantly without breaking the continuity of his development in any way. All of his theology is, at one and the same time, concrete and speculative, dogmatic and moral and, we might add, spiritual as well. We must be cautious about applying to the *Summa* categories that are not his. Whoever wishes to study Saint Thomas will quickly find himself needing to change his theological method.

The *Summa*

Structures and Content II

THE THIRD VOLUME, also known as the *Secunda Secundae,* has, among its peculiarities, that of being the longest. Its author considered it important enough to preface it with a Prologue, which is also the longest of the *Summa*. While helpful for the reader, it also contains a subtle warning. If Master Thomas, known for his concision, takes the pains to be more explicit, we have much to gain by following his explanations carefully.

THE VIRTUES AND THE VICES

The beginning of the Prologue is exactly what one would expect: "After studying the virtues and the vices in general as well as other points concerning morality, we must now consider each point in particular." In a few words, Thomas connects this part with the *Prima Secundae* and, as he did in the Second Part, lays out the material in two stages. The most interesting point, however, is what follows: "in morality, in fact, generalities are not very helpful, given that actions are comprised of particularities." From this it is clear that when the theologian considers human action, he must expect to confront an infinity of circumstances.

Before all else, then, he must ask himself how to proceed in an orderly fashion. He writes:

> In morality we can come to study the particular in two ways. One way is from the moral matter itself; for example, when we study this or that virtue or vice. The other way is from certain special circumstances; for example, when we study rulers and their subjects, those engaged in the active life and those in the contemplative, or any other category of persons. Therefore, we will first deal with what pertains to persons regardless of their situation; second, with what concerns particular situations (IIa IIae, Prol.).

This first division places the treatise on particular situations at the end of the volume (IIa IIae qq. 171–89), while the Prologue introduces what immediately follows. The first thing Thomas says, which seems to be simple good sense, is, in fact, full of significance:

> It should be said that if we wanted to study separately the virtues, the gifts [of the Holy Spirit], the vices, and the precepts, we would be prey to numerous repetitions. For example, whoever wishes to treat fully of the following precept: "Thou shall not commit adultery," must first inquire into adultery, which is a certain sin, and into the virtue which is opposed to it, for knowledge of the former depends on knowledge of it. Methodologically speaking, it will be easier and more fitting if, in the same treatise, we proceed from the virtue to the corresponding gift, then to the opposing vices, and finally to the positive and negative precepts. This method will befit the vices themselves according to their proper species. For, as we have shown already (Ia IIae q. 72), vices and sins differ among themselves according to their matter or object and not according to other differences such as being sins of thought, of word or of deed, or even of weakness, of ignorance or of malice, etc. In fact, it is according to the same matter that virtue acts rightly and that the opposing vices lead us away from rectitude (IIa IIae, Prol.).

Let us note in passing the beginning of this text. The failure of the manuals used at Orvieto lay precisely in placing the virtues and vices one after the other. It was to avoid this unnecessary repetition that Thomas undertook the writing of the *Summa* to begin with. Rather than piling up unhelpful information, Thomas offers his students a strong and well-ordered framework without which they would never master the considerable amount of material contained in this part. We should also carefully note the guiding principle he uses: virtues, gifts, vices, and precepts are dealt with in relationship to the same object but from different points of view. Specialists speak here of "specification by the object." Truth is attained through the understanding; the good, by the will. Both are specified by their proper object. The virtue of charity is specified by the proper love of God and neighbor. A lack of charity also concerns the love of God and neighbor, but the true relationship is falsified by selfishness or some other defect. In both cases, the same object specifies the act; its morality comes from elsewhere, namely, from the end pursued by the acting subject and from the circumstances surrounding the act.

A MORALITY OF VIRTUES

We do not have to wait long for the consequence of this fundamental option: "thus all of morality is brought back to the study of the virtues." We can understand without much explanation what results from the following simple observation. If the fact of placing happiness at the beginning already marks all of moral reflection with a focus towards the Good in itself, it is clear that an account of all that favors the pursuit of this Good will be first. The concrete obstacles that may be encountered in this pursuit, about which we will also speak, will never be the primary focus of Thomas's discourse. Thomas Aquinas's morality of virtues, governed by beatitude, gives rise to a Christian life that is resolutely oriented toward the positive.

From a theoretical perspective, this primary option is immediately expressed in the structure of the *Summa*. Since all of morality is brought back to the study of the virtues, "all of the virtues for their part must be brought back to seven: the three theological virtues which we will deal with first [qq. 1–46] and the four cardinal virtues which will follow" [qq. 47–170]. The reason for this division is clear: first, he treats the virtues that have God as their immediate object, followed by those that directly regulate action in concrete existence. This general approach is complemented by other reasons that govern the overall structure, first among which is the distinction between the intellectual and the moral virtues. Not all of them are cardinal virtues.

Among the intellectual virtues there is prudence which is also included among the cardinal virtues. But art [an intellectual virtue], which is the right rule of "doing," does not belong to morality, which is concerned with "acting," as we have said previously [Ia IIae q. 57 aa. 3–4]. As for the other three intellectual virtues: wisdom, understanding and knowledge, they share in common, even to their names, certain gifts of the Holy Spirit. That is why we will study them with the gifts that correspond to these virtues. As for the other moral virtues, all of them can be reduced in one way or another to the cardinal virtues as I have shown elsewhere [Ia IIae q. 61 a. 3]. Thus in studying each of the cardinal virtues, we will also study all of the virtues that are connected to them in some way as well as their opposing vices. Therefore nothing will be omitted from our study of morality (IIa IIae, Prol.).

Thomas says too many things in these few lines for us to see immediately all of their implications. But since my goal is to help people to read the *Summa,* I should draw the reader's attention to a particularity of this text that recurs frequently. Twice Thomas refers us to another passage: "as I have said previously." This scholarly way of speaking is a little heavy, but is necessary, and we should consider it carefully. Given the length of the *Summa* and always careful to avoid needless repetition, the author constantly refers back to what he has already said. If the reader does not do this, he will miss something essential. More than a mere detail, this difference between modern monographs and medieval Summas is a major one, and the casual reader is regularly misled by it. Because books of today are focused on a particular point, they can bring together almost everything that can be said about its subject. By contrast, medieval works, because they synthesize a greater amount of material, are of necessity more succinct and require more sustained attention. Once certain developments have been introduced in their proper place, medieval authors do not feel compelled to discuss the matter again, preferring to refer the reader to its previous development. It is not enough then to consult the subject index of the *Summa* to learn if it treats of one subject or another, for the subjects treated can be found in diverse places where the reader would never dream to look. The Church's theology offers a well known example: we find it in connection with Christ and the sacraments but also in the treatise on the new law and even throughout the Second Part.

Major Themes of This Second Stage

The Prologue introduced the major themes of this volume. Now we must look at the content. Space does not permit a detailed analysis, but I will try to highlight the most important elements of both treatises.

Thomas begins with an account of the theological virtues. They are called this for three reasons: God *(theos)* is their object; God is also their sole cause; God alone reveals to us their existence. In accordance with the order received from ancient catechesis, Thomas treats successively faith, by which "eternal life has already begun in us" (qq. 1–16); hope, by which "we dare to hope from God nothing less than God himself" (qq. 17–22); charity, by which we reach perfection, "for it unites us to God who is our final end" (qq. 23–46).

The three theological virtues have much in common. They are clearly grouped around the virtue of faith: God is its sole "material" and "formal" object. He is the "material" object of faith ("essential" might be more meaningful for us) because he is the first content of faith and what we believe. We believe that God is the first truth insofar as he is our salvation. He is the "formal" object of faith because he is the one *by whom* we believe. It is he who witnesses to our spirit that he is the truth. Thomas affirms this forcefully from the very beginning of his treatise (q. 1 a. 1). This is all the more noteworthy because in his previous treatments of faith (in the *Sentences* and in *De veritate*), he began with the interior act of faith of the believer and ended with the *object* of that faith. Here he does the inverse. This is his way of saying that it is not faith that creates the object but the contrary: God, by his word, makes himself known and arouses in man assent to that word and a surrender of self to it, a total abandonment to the Person who speaks. Thomas summarizes this in three phrases: to believe *God (credere Deum),* to believe in *God (credere Deo),* to believe *in God (credere in Deum).* Although the first two expressions are sufficient for intellectual adherence, the third stresses the fact that faith is a living assent, penetrated by love, in which the entire person is implicated and where God is as much loved as—and even better loved than—known (q. 2 a. 2). The stress on God as the sole object of faith does not, of course, exclude Christ or his work of salvation. Far from overlooking Christ, Thomas clearly explains his necessary presence in the beatific vision as well as in faith. He writes:

> Realities that, as such, belong to faith are those that will, when we see them, cause us to rejoice in eternal life and those by which we are led to it. Two things will be presented for our contemplation: the divine secret, the vision of which will make us happy, and the mystery of the humanity of Christ, by whom we have access to *the freedom of the glory of the children of God* (Rom 5.2). This confirms what Saint John says (17.3): "Eternal life is knowing you, the one true God, and the one whom you sent, Jesus Christ" (q. 1 a. 8).

If lack of space allows me to say only one more thing concerning the theological virtues, it should be said about the virtue of charity. Of all the authors of his time, Thomas is alone in having the boldness to define charity as a friendship, that is, as a reciprocity of love between God and man founded on God's self-communication when, by grace, he makes man a participant in his own happiness (q. 23 a. 1). Struck by the use of the words *communio* and *communicatio* (*koinōnia* in the New Testament) to express the relationship that we have with God and by Aristotle's use of the same word to describe a friendship based on a total community between friends, Thomas does not hesitate to raise what the Greek philosopher had learned from human experience to the supernatural level of the love of God and neighbor. This deserves to be underlined for its exemplary value. Whoever wishes to study the contribution of ancient thought to Christian theology and the transformation of the former by the latter will find a case study here.

THE QUEEN OF THE CARDINAL VIRTUES

We cannot examine all of the virtues here, but neither can we neglect the central role of prudence. Current usage considers prudence to be a timorous attitude and rather negative. But in the *Summa,* prudence is the virtue of choice and decision, of personal responsibility, of risks consciously taken. It belongs to prudence to bring to conclusion the deliberative process, by proposing a course of action in a specific, unique, and unrepeatable situation. There is no room for hesitation here:

Prudence is the most necessary virtue of human life. To live well means to act well. Now to act well not only must we do something, but we must do it as we should, i.e., according to a well-ordered choice and not merely on impulse or through passion. But since choice has to do with the means to an end, its rectitude requires two things: a just end and means that are adapted to that just end. . . . Concerning the means, we must be directly prepared for them by means of a *habitus* of reason, for deliberation and choice—operations which belong to the means—are acts of reason. This is why *it is necessary that reason possess an intellectual virtue that gives it enough perfection to act well with respect to the means to be taken. This virtue is prudence. And this is why prudence is a necessary virtue to live well* (Ia IIae q. 57 a. 5).

This insistence is striking. Here we are at the cross-roads of the moral thought of Aquinas. Certainly every virtue is necessary in order "to live well," but it is to prudence that we look to give reason full place in practicing the virtues. The virtues are lived in human affectivity. This is why they are located in the will, which has the privilege of moving all of the other powers of the soul. Thomas fully recognizes this, but he also speaks unceasingly about the right regulation that reason must exercise over human life. "*Moral virtue* can certainly exist without certain intellectual virtues, for example, without wisdom, science or art, but it *cannot exist without understanding* [*intellectus: habitus* of the first principles] *or without prudence*" (Ia IIae q. 58 a. 4).

Acting requires that we grasp the means correctly in light of the end. This cannot be done except by a reason that knows how *to give good counsel, to judge,* and *to command,* which is the role of prudence and of the connected virtues. This does not mean that one need be a savant in order to be virtuous. Thomas is not Socrates, for whom it is the intellectual alone who lives morally to the extent that behavior depends on knowledge. But if Thomas does not want to identify virtue with right reason, neither does he want to reduce virtue to a purely irrational inclination to the good. This would be all the more dangerous because it is so powerful.

THE CONNECTION OF THE VIRTUES

If we are at a strategic place in Thomas's construction, it is because we find here his fundamental option for the substantial unity of the human person. Man is not simply intelligence more or less joined to the animality of his nature, nor is he pure will without intelligence or vice versa. This helps us to understand not only the central place that Thomas gives to prudence but also another important thesis for him: the harmony or the "connection" of the virtues under the aegis of prudence. He writes: "*We can have no moral virtue without prudence. . . . Similarly, we cannot have prudence without the moral virtues*" (Ia IIae q. 65 a. 1).

This thesis is not in itself new. Thomas inherited it from the patristic tradition. But with Thomas it has a new demand and force. Virtue "renders good" the one who possesses it; it builds the virtuous person. But it is the subject himself who acts by the virtues. Virtues, far from ignoring each other, intervene in the work of other virtues, giving each other mutual aid, each having need of another to attain its end. Their harmony is precisely the work of prudence, but it must be added that prudence is not itself except in its connection with charity. With his expression *credere in Deum,* Thomas already made it clear that the theological virtues of faith and hope are only truly themselves when they are penetrated by charity. The same can be said of the cardinal virtues: if they are truly to be virtues, not only must they be connected to prudence, they must also be "informed" by charity. One is not brave, just, or temperate if one is not prudent; one is not as prudent as one should be if one does not love. Thomas is so convinced of this that he hesitates to speak of *true* virtue except where grace intervenes (at least anonymously). There are as many infused virtues as there are virtues that are naturally possible. This means that grace and charity are omnipresent in all virtuous activity.

Prudence, therefore, is not the only virtue at work when the person acts. What is proper to prudence, however, is its architectonic role. It is prudence that provides the directing activity of reason in the entire domain of acting. The three other moral virtues which, like prudence, are also cardinal virtues, will complete prudence's task according to the general area of action assigned to them to rectify. First of all, there is the area of relationships with other people. This is the sphere of *justice,* which has as its proper object the objective ordering of activities with respect to what we owe others, be they persons or society (qq. 57–122). Next comes the area of personal discipline, that is, the relationship of the person to his affective reactions, his passions. Whether the matter concerns strengthening one's resolution or confronting an obstacle, that is, facing whatever could turn one away from the good either because of laziness or fear, the person will need the virtue of *fortitude* (qq. 123–40). When it comes to resisting everything that can separate us from the good because of easy pleasure, we must restrain and moderate ourselves. For this we need the fourth cardinal virtue, that of temperance (qq. 141–70).

PARTICULAR SITUATIONS

The above considerations occupy most of the third volume of the *Summa*. Everything that we have just covered applies to everyone, regardless of his state in life. If we continue reading, we come to "that which concerns specifically certain categories of persons" (qq. 171–89). Thomas returns to and develops this brief idea taken from the general Prologue, explaining that from this new point of view, we can notice three types of differences. In the first place, we have the differences that arises from the diversity of "graces freely given," that is to say, charisms, which are listed in the New Testament: prophecy, rapture, tongues, miracles (qq. 171–78). In the second place, we have the diversity of forms of life which, in turn, leads to a discussion of the great distinction between the active and the contemplative lives (qq. 179–82). Finally, we have the diversity of functions (today we would speak of "ministries") and states of life in the Church. Here, Thomas speaks of the episcopacy and the religious life (qq. 183–89).

All that Thomas speaks of in this last section is of the highest interest from an ecclesiological point of view, but what concerns the religious life is of special importance. In these pages, which provide us with the final stage of his thinking on this subject, Thomas explains once again and defends with vigor the ideal of his religious order. Particularly inspiring in this context is the formula that he forged and in which the Dominicans like to see their motto but which, in reality, applies to whoever places himself at the service of the Word of God: to transmit to others what one has contemplated (*contemplata aliis tradere;* q. 188 a. 6).

The Third Part

Now we turn our attention to the fourth volume which contains the Third Part of the *Summa.* It is entirely consecrated to Christ and to his work of salvation. Many authors have expressed surprise that Thomas waited until the last part of his work to speak of Christ, as if he had forgotten him and now comes back to repair his mistake. This surprise—which is sometimes expressed as a reproach—proceeds from a misunderstanding that is easily clarified if we understand the circular pattern about which I have already spoken. Sometimes this pattern is read simplistically, as if the "going out from" belongs to the *Prima Pars* (which is inexact) and that of the "return" to the *Secunda Pars* (we stop too soon). So we do not know what to do with the *Tertia Pars* and that is why it is seen as an irreducible addition.

A REVIEW OF THE STRUCTURE OF THE 'SUMMA'

In fact, the situation is more nuanced. The tripartite division announced at the beginning of the *Summa* corresponds to real in-

ternal necessities, but this division does not say everything regarding the plan of the whole. Upon this tripartite division is su-
perimposed another—this one bipartite—which has the advantage of correcting what could have been an overly material and
separating reading. The bipartite division suggests a more unified
vision of things, by means of which we can better grasp the general dynamic of the work.

This division into two parts retrieves a distinction that is familiar to the Fathers of Church between "theology"—the consideration of God in himself: Trinitarian theology—and "econo-
my"—the work of God as it is accomplished in time, that is,
salvation history. In fact, this is what the Prologue at the beginning of the *Summa* (Ia q. 2) announces: Thomas's intention is to
transmit doctrine concerning God, first as he is in himself
(which is the object of questions 2 through 43 of the First Part);
then as he is the principle and end of all things (this covers *the
rest of the work*—not only the first, but also the Second and Third
Parts).

The circular schema of "going out from" and "returning to"
God, the Alpha and Omega, applies only to the "economic" part
of the *Summa*. The movement of the "going out from" corresponds to the end of the First Part (qq. 44–119). Thomas begins
as the Bible does, with the creation in time: "In the beginning
God created the heavens and the earth." The complementary
movement is described in the Second and Third Parts. These
parts are perfectly unified under the sign of the "return" of the
rational creature to God under the leadership of Christ. The incarnate Word takes the lead in this movement for he alone is
able to bring it to completion. The whole project is brought
(ought to have been brought) to completion at the end of the
Third Part by the glorious return of Christ at the end of time

and the beginning of new heavens and a new earth. Between the two creations is placed the entire history of salvation in its diverse stages. Thomas can thus integrate the historical and existential evolution of the work of God in a perfectly organic way within a harmonious structure that, of itself, helps us to understand his project.

Christ

This is the perspective that we find in the Prologue to the Third Part:

Our Savior, the Lord Jesus . . . showed himself to us as the *way* of the *truth* by which it is now possible for us to arrive at the resurrection and the happiness of immortal *life*. Thus *to bring to completion our entire theological task, it is necessary*, after having studied the final end of human life, then the virtues and the vices, *to continue our study with the Savior of all* considered in himself, followed by the benefits with which he has graced humankind (IIIa Prol.).

This text makes it clear that for Master Thomas, Christ occupies as central a place in his theology as he does in the Christian life. John 14.9 reminds us of Christ's place in the Christian life when he writes that Christ, the *way*, the *truth*, and the *life*, is the one who allows access to beatitude. Thomas cannot be more clear: the study of Christ is *necessary* to achieve the goal of his theological enterprise.

The conclusion of the text makes clear Thomas's approach. Here once again, Thomas presents the divisions and subdivisions as a manner of course, helping us to see the structure that he proposes. The first subdivision, which is about Jesus the Christ, the Savior who brings us salvation (qq. 1–59), is subdivided into two large sections: the mystery of the Incarnation in itself (qq. 1–26) and what the Word did and suffered for us in the flesh (qq. 27–59). The second subdivision is made up of a study of the sacraments by which we achieve salvation: first, in general (qq. 60–65), then Baptism, the Eucharist, and Penance (qq. 60–90). As we know, Thomas's death impeded him from finishing this treatise on the sacraments and the *Summa* itself remained unfinished. But we must not forget the third subdivision, already anticipated and announced, which would have treated in considerable detail the final end to which we are called and the eternal life that we will enter by rising through and in Christ.

REASONS OF APPROPRIATENESS

The first question asks about the "appropriateness" of the incarnation of the Word. This term deserves a closer look, for it expresses both a spiritual attitude and a theological method. Master Thomas holds with the Bible the certainty that the work of God in the world is pregnant with meaning accessible to human reason. Since "God has regulated all things with number, weight and measure" (Wis 11.20), and since he has disposed all things "with wisdom and understanding" (Eph 1.8), it must be possible for the theologian to discover and understand something of the way in which things work in God's plan. Not that God wills "this" because of "that" (no necessity is ever imposed on God), but he does will "that this be because of that" (Ia q. 19 a. 5).

If we could characterize the originality of this proposition with one word, we would speak of the ostensive function of theology (*ostendere:* to show). Contrary to a deductive method that is sometimes attributed to him but which is not his, Thomas does not want to prove the truths of the faith, nor to demonstrate other truths from those that he holds in faith. He simply wants to bring to the fore the connections that bind together the truths that we do hold and to show how all of this is explained as coming from God. This, ultimately, is the meaning of the overall schema of "going out from" and "returning to." But within this overall schema there is room for an infinity of other relations that the theologian tries to bring to the fore by reasons that have an explanatory value with respect to each other. For example, from faith's certainty that Christ is resurrected, Thomas asserts that the resurrection of Christ will be the cause of our own resurrection (Ia q. 1 a. 8). We already hold these two truths in faith, and their relationship does not prove one with respect to the other. We simply make explicit the second by the first, but we can still speak in this case of a rationally acquired certainty. When it comes to a primary truth, for example the incarnation of the Word, reason cannot arrive at a comparable certainty, but only at a rightness or, if one prefers, at an "appropriateness." When Thomas asks himself about the "why" of the Incarnation, and since clearly he cannot grant it any kind of necessity, he simply asks himself if it is "appropriate" for God to become incarnate. To try to make clear that to which this "appropriateness" responds, he appeals to what we know about God:

> The nature itself of God is the essence of goodness. . . . Thus everything that belongs to the nature of the good is appropriate to God. Now it is in the nature of the good to communicate itself to others. . . . Thus it belongs in the highest sense to the Sovereign Good to communicate himself. And this sovereign communication is realized, according to Saint Augustine, when God "joins himself to created nature in such a way as to form only one person in these three realities: the Word, the soul, and the flesh." The appropriateness of the Incarnation is thus evident (IIIa q. 1 a 1).

This line of reasoning, to be well understood, must be read within the framework of Thomas's synthesis. It is in the nature of the good to communicate itself, but this by no means implies that God is constrained to diffuse his goodness. His freedom remains intact. It is precisely God's freedom that "appropriateness" respects, thus expressing a spiritual attitude of respect for the mystery. But it is also a theological method, since the theologian, to be true to himself, cannot refuse the challenge of trying to understand the mystery. He thus tries to give as many reasons as he can, in spite of their weaknesses, to grasp all that he can of the incomprehensible love that moved God to this extreme.

THE HUMANITY OF CHRIST

It is with this in mind that Thomas divides his study into several subsections which, little by little, lay out the diverse aspects of Christ's ontology and psychology. First comes the section on the hypostatic union itself, which studies the diverse facets of the mystery of the union of the human and the divine nature in the unity of the person of the Word (qq. 2–6). Here Thomas shows himself to be quite well informed about the great patristic and conciliar tradition which developed the dogmatic teachings on Christ over the course of several centuries. He is the first in the West to know and to use the complete collection of the early councils. Between the writing of the *Sentences* and the *Tertia Pars,* his references to this tradition saw a six-fold increase. Well aware of the various controversies, he made full use not only of the teachings of the school of Antioch and of Saint Leo the Great, from whom the Council of Chalcedon (in 451) retained the most important elements, but also of those of Cyril of Alexandria at Ephesus (431) as reread by the Second Council of Constantinople (553).

With the grace with which the humanity of Christ is endowed, Thomas begins a new sub-section on the *coassumpta,* that
is to say, those realities, both perfections and limitations, that the
Word co-assumed at the same time that he assumed a concrete
human nature. Then, two questions examine the role of grace in
Christ: the personal dimension (sanctifying grace, the gifts of the
Holy Spirit, charisms [q. 7]); the social dimension (grace was not
given to Christ as a private person but as the head of the
Church; this is why we speak of a "capital" grace [q. 8]). A theology of the Church that wanted to take its inspiration from the
Summa would find in this second question some critical elements.

Continuing with the perfections of Christ, Thomas asserts
that his soul was endowed with knowledge and power (qq.
9–13). The first of these two qualities raises more questions than
it answers. Theology has, as its starting point, this one fact: Christ
was God and, as such, he possessed the uncreated knowledge of
the Word. But this does not obviate the need for his created soul
to know things by means of his human faculties. Were this not
the case, his humanity would have known nothing at all and
would have been assumed by the Word in vain (q. 9). Thomas
grants, therefore, three kinds of knowledge to the soul of Christ:
the beatific vision by which he could see God in the same way
that the elect of heaven do (q. 10); infused knowledge by which
he had knowledge of all that can be known by human intelligence (q. 11); and finally acquired knowledge by which he knew
the same way all men know, from experience (q. 12).

This last point, which seems obvious to us, was not so in the
thirteenth century. Thomas was the only theologian to say it and
even his own thinking evolved on the subject since, in the *Sen-*

tences, he was still in accord with the common opinion. The other two points were held by all. The logic of this development of the knowledge of God became common currency in Catholic theology until the twentieth century. With some fine-tuning, a number of Thomist theologians still hold to this way of looking at the issue. Many more, no doubt, whether Thomists or not, contest this view. In my opinion, and in keeping with the example of Thomas himself, who evolved appreciably and was not afraid to admit it, it is possible to retain some of his contributions, but it is not the time to enter into this discussion.

After discussing the perfections, Thomas goes on to consider the *defectus* of Christ's humanity. For Thomas, these clearly do not denote "faults," nor are they really "deficiencies" (which, in our language, suggests imperfection). They are, rather, the concrete conditions of assuming a human nature and are best referred to as "limits." Since Christ assumed a concrete human nature, we can expect not only that he is capable of suffering (q. 14) but also that he is subject to the same emotions (i.e., to "passions" in the language of the *Summa*) as we (q. 15). Thomas admits, then, the full humanity of Christ who was subject to pain, sadness, astonishment, and anger. But in keeping with Scripture, he does not ascribe to him the presence of sin any more than he does concupiscence which, in us, is the residue of original sin. This is why Thomas says that Christ voluntarily assumed suffering and death but does not say that he was subject to them. Since Christ was totally free from sin, he was not subject to them in the same way that we are.

We can sometimes have the impression that Thomas does not see his intuitions through to the end. But his study of the passions of Christ is one of those chapters that best dispels any notion of docetism. In the following sub-section, he discusses the unity of Christ's being (q. 17), the manner in which his human freedom submits to the divine will (q. 18), and the way in which these two distinct operations of his two natures come together in one concrete action (divino-human or theandric). These considerations, in spite of their speculative difficulty, are also of capital importance.

Now that we have understood Christ's human freedom, Thomas develops the notion of the instrumentality of his humanity. This he gets directly from the Greek patristic tradition and it has a rich meaning for Christian life. It means that the grace that comes from the Holy Spirit as its first source is "colored" in some sense by passing through Christ with all of the qualities that are his. This grace, having received his imprint, is then communicated to his body, the Church and becomes properly Christian, making of those who receive it prophets, priests, and kings. The following two sub-sections can be read from this perspective and suggest the consequences of this union, first, with respect to his Father: submission, prayer, priesthood, sonship, and predestination (qq. 20–24); then, with respect to us: his adoration and his mediation between God and humanity (qq. 25–26).

THE "MYSTERIES" OF CHRIST'S LIFE

The second large section of the *Summa*'s Christology is spread out over thirty-three questions, one for each year of Christ's life. This is why it is sometimes called—wrongly, but not without reason—"the Life of Christ." It is divided into four clearly marked subsections. First, the entrance *(ingressus)* of Christ into the world, which runs from the sanctification of the Virgin Mary in the womb of her mother to Jesus's baptism by John the Baptist, by way of Mary's virginity and marriage, the Annunciation, the child's conception and birth, . . . (qq. 27–39). Second, the unfolding *(processus)* of Christ's life in which Thomas looks at his manner of life, temptations, teaching, miracles, and transfiguration (qq. 40–45). Third, his leaving *(exitus)* the world, which includes his passion (with a study of the responsibility of those who decided it, its efficacy and its salvific fruits), his entombment, and his descent into Hell (qq. 46–52). Lastly, his exaltation, that is, his resurrection (including the modes of existence and appearances of the risen Christ, as well as the way in which his resurrection remains efficacious in our world), his ascension, his exaltation at the right hand of the Father, and how he will judge the living and the dead (qq. 53–59).

We cannot, unfortunately, explore every detail, but we can at least glimpse the astonishing richness of this section in this simple enumeration. Let us select three features that are important for the practice of theology to look at more closely.

First, here once again, Thomas embarks on new ground. He is neither the first nor the only medieval theologian to speak of the life of Christ and of his great saving work, but he is the first and the only to treat them within a structured unity conceived of as an integral part of his speculative Christology. While other authors refer to them occasionally, in order to stress the humanity of Christ for example, Thomas looks at them from the perspective of ontology and soteriology (from the Greek *sōtēr:* Savior) as well.

Second, we should note that Thomas is not writing a biography (this is why the expression "the life of Christ" is not accurate). Rather, his intention is to write about the "mysteries" of

the life of Christ, his task being to develop theologically what
"Christ did and suffered while in the flesh" [*acta et passa Christi
in carne*]. If we speak of "mysteries," it is to make clear that each
of the events that marked the life of the Word made flesh, from
his birth to his resurrection, is conceived of as a manifestation
and a realization in act of the total *mysterion* in the Pauline sense
of that word (Rom 16.25 f.; cf. Eph 3.1–13).

The third and final feature is one that the reader may have
already noticed. This part of the *Summa* is constructed according
to three time periods mirroring the very unfolding of Jesus's life:
his entrance into the world *(ingressus),* his life in the world
(processus), his leaving the world *(exitus).* The fourth and final
stage begun by the Resurrection is his life in glory. This schema
is that of the *Summa* as a whole; only the vocabulary changes
slightly. The path followed by Jesus is in fact that of all creation
and is, therefore, the path that we must take to be with him in
paradise. Thus Thomas establishes the exemplary value of the
mysteries of the life of Jesus, making this treatise one of the
places where we can best grasp the connection between his theology and the spiritual life.

The Sacraments

Thomas introduces the second sub-part of the *Tertia Pars* with
his usual concision: "After the study of the mysteries of the incarnate Word comes that of the sacraments of the Church, for it
is from the incarnate Word that they have their efficacy" (q. 60,
Prol.). This treatise is organized around two main considerations.
The first concerns those general conditions valid for all of the
sacraments: definition (q. 60), necessity (q. 61), effects (qq. 62–

63), cause (q. 64), number (q. 65). The second examines each sacrament individually and in particular: Baptism (qq. 66–71), Confirmation (q. 72), the Eucharist (qq. 73–83), Penance (qq. 84–90). The list stops here since, as we already know, Thomas's death interrupted his work.

This treatise presupposes two important pieces of information. On the one hand, even though Thomas seems to be introducing a new category, in reality what we have here is a simple modality of the over-arching category of "means" discussed at the beginning of the *Prima Pars*. It is not only the free acts of man that lead him to beatitude; God also took measures to assist him by giving him the law, grace, and now the sacraments, which are the means par excellence of grace. In some respects, the sacraments are acts of man that stem from the virtue of religion, since they are acts of worship. But they are also and before all else acts of Christ, from whom they derive their efficacy.

A SANCTIFYING REALITY

The brief introduction to the treatise reminds us of the sanctifying reality of the sacraments. Their efficacy comes from the efficacy of Christ the God-man. Thomas's study of the sacraments does not come, therefore, until after he has dealt with Christ in his being and action as the ultimate form under which comes to us the salvation begun by the earthly acts of Christ. This has been immortalized in an immense sculpture of Christ on the doors of the church at Vezelay. There the sacraments are depicted as rays that come forth from him, meeting the world of men at his feet, his hands meeting us through time and space.

To account for this salutary efficacy Thomas had to be precise in formulating his definition. In keeping with the etymolo-

gy that came to him from Augustine, he fully admits that the
sacrament is a sacred sign. But he does not think this sufficient
to explain the redeeming fruitfulness that the sign carries. Neither does he use the abbreviated formula frequently used after
him of "an efficacious sign" for, clearly, the sign is not efficacious in the sense that it produces something. Rather, its proper
way of acting is to signify. Thomas's definition of sacrament,
therefore, brings together both meaning and efficacy in one formula: "the sign of a sacred reality that is acting to sanctify man"
(q. 60 a. 2). It is not the sign that acts but the reality of grace that
it signifies and, supremely, the author of grace himself: Christ
who acts through the sacraments in the great sacrament which
is the Church herself.

The mention of the Church in this context is not accidental.
The doctrine of the sacraments is one of those privileged places
where we grasp better Thomas's understanding of the Church
(the other places, the reader will recall, are to be found in his
Christology and in his theology of the Holy Spirit). A number
of texts repeat that the Church is "founded," "built," "constitut-
ed," "made" by faith and the sacraments of the faith. Behind
these expressions, we can discern the rich patristic theme of the
birth of the Church on the Cross. Blood and water flowing out
from the pierced side of Christ is interpreted, both in the East
and in the West, as the symbol of baptism and the Eucharist.
Now, if baptism is what joins us to the Body of Christ which is
the Church, Thomas insists on the ultimate fruit of the Eucharist, which is not merely a grace of intimacy with Christ, but
also the unity of the ecclesial body.

BODY AND SPIRIT

Another characteristic of this theology is a fruitful analogy between bodily life and sacramental life. While his contemporaries justified the seven sacraments by establishing a correlation with the seven capital sins (Albert the Great), or with the three theological virtues and the four cardinal virtues (Bonaventure), Thomas seems unique in establishing a parallel between bodily life and the spiritual life. This seems more natural and more rich. Besides birth, he underscores the notion of growth which is the law of human life. This growth has two dimensions: "[Life] has two kinds of perfection: one pertaining to the person himself, the other pertaining to the social community in which he lives, for man is by nature a social animal" (q. 65 a. 1). The relation of man to the entire community is evidenced in the supreme fruit of the Eucharist that is the unity of the mystical body and in two additional ways. First, by the authority who governs the many through the exercise of public functions. That which corresponds to this in the life of the Church is the sacrament of Orders, since priests do not offer the Eucharist only for themselves but for all the people. Second, since this social end is realized through the natural propagation of the species, the human person is perfected through Marriage as much bodily as spiritually, since marriage, before being a sacrament, is a natural institution. Thomas also sees another relationship between the sacramental body and the ecclesial body in the fact that the sacraments are the foundation of Church law.

The Uncompleted End

The treatment of the movement of the return of man to God should have ended as it had begun, with a study of the final end. Between these two treatments of the end, Thomas placed his reflections on concrete human acts and on all that God did for man in his incarnate Word in order to bring about this end. The idea of beatitude (i.e., life in communion with the living God, a life already begun by grace), present and operative throughout this entire process, is the exact theological translation of an eschatology in the process of being realized as we find it in the New Testament. By placing the study of the recapitulation of all things in Jesus Christ at the end of his work, Thomas accomplishes his task, which is to rediscover, in light of what he learned from revelation, the internal intelligibility of the Mystery and of its dispensation in time.

We are not without information concerning what would have been the content of the third sub-part. His disciples tried to complete the work of their master by borrowing, from parallel passages in his commentary on the *Sentences,* those elements that seemed to belong there. This *Supplement,* as it is called, was written with good intentions and with reasonable success, and it does provide a quantity of important information. But it is preferable to read these passages in the work from which they were borrowed or, at least, to remember that they were written twenty years earlier. In what we have, we find no trace of the progress that we see in the first pages of this Third Part. In the new conclusions he had reached with respect to the positions he took as a younger man, Thomas leaves his reader and disciple an example of his unceasing journey in search of the truth.

The Literary and Doctrinal Milieu

N OW THAT WE HAVE MET THE *Summa's* author and come to know its major features as well as the essential elements of its content, there remains the task of saying something about the milieu in which it was written. While suggestive, evoking Thomas's experience at Orvieto is too fleeting and fragmentary to be helpful. That experience is situated against a historical and cultural background that will be useful to bear in mind. Thomas is a man of his time, a time that we cannot completely understand apart from the intellectual ferment of his century, with its knowledge, its discoveries, and its preoccupations. Without venturing to recreate the many excellent works that continue to expand our knowledge of this fascinating culture, we must nonetheless call to mind those things that can help us to understand the *Summa theologiae* better.

Literary Panorama

First of all, it is important to take note of the fact that the *Summa* corresponds to only one of four principal literary genres of the theological milieux of the Middle Ages. Three of them come directly from oral teaching: the commentary on the Bible, the commentary on the *Sentences*, and the disputed questions. The various Summas, which are situated against this background, are not directly the result of oral teaching. In any case, Thomas's *Summa* was not taught. It was only much later that it would become itself the object of commentaries.

"LECTURA"

The "lectura" is the first kind of literary genre used in teaching. In every discipline, the basic method consisted in "reading" line-by-line the works of ancient and recognized authors, the "authorities," and in providing as needed the explanations necessary to understand them. The course was therefore called *lectio* and the explanation was called *lectura*. The noun "lecturer" used in certain languages has its origin in this practice. Whether the course concerned grammar with Priscian, philosophy with Aristotle, law with the two juridical *corpus,* or theology with the Bible and the Sentences, the procedure was always the same. To assist him, the teacher often used annotated copies in which were found the most important explanations of the preceding tradition.

The best known example is that of the Bible, completely annotated by the school of Anselm of Laon at the beginning of the twelfth century but which had already given place much earlier to this kind of commentary. We find the origins of it in the patristic commentaries on the sacred text. The florilegia or "chains" of quotations from the Fathers, which appeared very early on, were the preferred materials for these annotations. While they were not always firsthand materials, they nonetheless contributed to the transmission of an important part of the heritage of the first centuries.

In Thomas's time, two kinds of this type of teaching were known. The first, the "cursive" reading, is what the bachelor of biblical studies did. Rapid by definition, this method was but the first approach and often limited itself to indicating the divisions of the text and to a few literary explanations. This kind of commentary is not very satisfying to the modern reader, even when it comes to a work of quality such as the *Super Isaiam*. The other kind of reading, *lectura* or *expositio,* was reserved for the master, who provided a more in-depth commentary, drawing on diverse patristic authorities, whose differences he did not hesitate to point out and on the basis of which he often raised questions.

QUESTIONS AND QUODLIBETS

With the commentary on Scripture, the Question (which became little by little "disputed") is the second major mode of university teaching. Its origins can be found in the middle of the twelfth century with authors such as Robert of Melun and Odo of Soissons. Initially, the Question simply took the form of a slightly fuller development within the context of the commentary on the Bible with respect to a given difficulty: "Here a question can be raised" [*Hic oritur quaestio*].

Toward the end of the century, with Simon of Tournai, the Question became a scholarly exercise in itself and took the place of a Master's lecture. At the very beginning of the thirteenth century, we have the Questions of Stephen Langton. But the definitive appearance of this genre in the university did not occur until between 1215 and 1231. The Question quickly took the form of a regular exercise (the *ordinary* disputed question), which took place on a Saturday every fortnight. The frequency of this exercise soon became burdensome and the masters gladly got themselves out of taking part in it, whence the regulations requiring their participation.

The *extraordinary* debates, called Quodlibets, appeared later (although Thomas was already engaged in them beginning in 1256) and were held twice a year, at Easter and Christmas. Even though the masters did not always want to participate in these debates, the public was fond of them, for their tournament-like atmosphere made of them a much-appreciated spectacle. As they often dealt with current events (or at least contained elements that were about current events), they are still today of enormous importance for the history of the university at that time.

Whether ordinary or solemn, the Question always consists of at least five elements. (1) First comes a very brief preamble consisting of an exposition of the question that the master submits for discussion. This can be for internal use for students who are introduced to a given subject and, by closely examining it, deepen their knowledge while at the same time perfecting their debating skills. Or it can be for a public meeting in which masters and students of other schools participate. (2) Then comes a series of arguments in support of the thesis under discussion. (3) This is followed by a series of counter-arguments. This *pro et contra* series of exchanges has as its aim to advance the search for a solution by means of a dialectical process. It is easy to see that these last two elements, while different from each other in the written form of the Question, were, in fact, intermingled in reality. (4) After this comes the *determinatio magistralis,* that is, the detailed response given by the master to the question that he himself posed and that was usually postponed until another session (in the afternoon, if the discussion took place in the morning, or the following morning, or even another day). (5) Finally, there are the responses to the objections raised in the previous discussion.

It is very important for the reader of the *Summa* to be familiar with this structure, for *all* of the articles are constructed according to this schema. What was originally simply the reflection of a more or less animated oral discussion became a process of personal reflecting on and writing about. Even works that had not been taught orally were written according to this procedure of stating a problem, followed by questions and answers, and concluding with questions and solutions. Antiquity favored the "dialogical" style (Augustine also practiced it, following the example of Plato). Master Thomas, like all medieval scholastics, thought and wrote according to the disputed question mode.

We need only look at any article of the *Summa* to find this structure. (1) The question proposed for the debate is always found at the beginning and is usually stated in terms of a pedagogical doubt raised by the master: "It seems that [*videtur quod*] sacred doctrine is not a science" (Ia q. 1 a. 2). (2) There follow three or four reasons that give rise to a negative response. (3) Then comes the argument "but on the contrary," the *sed contra,* which serves as a kind of safety catch to the series of opposing arguments and also introduces the position that the master will take. Usually the *sed contra* is an "authority": Scripture or one of the Fathers of the Church. (4) Thomas then proposes his position in a slightly more developed form: "Response" *(Responsio)* in the body of the article. (5) Last, there follow the detailed responses to each of the difficulties that had been raised. (It should now be clear that this structure is used in citing the *Summa;* thus Ia q. 1 a. 2 *resp.* should be read as: *Prima Pars,* question 1, article 2, response—or, as the case may be: *obj.* or *arg.* 1 [objection 1 or argument 1]; *ad* 1 [response to the first objection]; and so on.)

In order to read these articles profitably, one should keep in mind a few simple facts. First of all, one should never lose sight of the fact that the unifying principle is not the article but the question. The articles dissect the different problems that arise with respect to one question. It is only after reading the different problems that we will arrive at the complete and nuanced response of the author. In the example I previously used, "What is sacred doctrine?" (Ia q. 1), Thomas raises no fewer than ten different problems, which he discusses in as many articles: what is its necessity? (a. 1); is it a science? (a. 2); a unique science? (a. 3); a practical science? (a. 4); what is its place among the other sciences? (a. 5); is it wisdom? (a. 6); what is its subject? (a. 7); does it proceed by rational argument? (a. 8); does it use metaphors? (a. 9); and finally, since it is identified in part with Scripture, what should we think about the multiple senses of Scripture? (a. 10).

In this simple example, the subject debated can be reduced to one question. This does not dispense with the need to look at parallel texts for mutual clarification (it happens sometimes that Thomas is clearer or more complete in other works). In addition, there are ensembles of questions that have been titled "treatises." In this case, even if each question maintains its unity, and even if there are sub-groupings of questions that constitute intermediate unities, clearly the whole treatise must be read, as one would a short book.

SENTENCES

It should be clear by now that even a summary description of the literary landscape of the thirteenth century cannot limit itself to talking only about the Summas. In fact, parallel to the disputed questions, the commentaries on the *Sentences* also made their appearance and soon took center stage on the university scene. The masters of the cathedral schools had commented on parts of the work of Peter Lombard very shortly after its writing. But not until Alexander of Hales was it used at the University of Paris (between 1223 and 1227; ed. Quaracchi, 1951–57). The Dominican Hugh of Saint-Cher followed soon after (from 1229–32: his teaching and writing; not yet edited) and, between 1243–45, it was the turn of Albert the Great. As for Bonaventure, he came just before Thomas (1250–52).

Toward the middle of the century, this exercise became mandatory for all future masters and took on such an importance that the Franciscan Roger Bacon (around 1270) became incensed to see the commentary on the *Sentences* supplanting that of Scripture. Thus, when the statutes of the Faculty of Theology were drawn up around 1335–36, they were only ratifying an already well-established usage. At that time and for a long time thereafter, the *Sentences* was the basic book for the study of theology. But with a major difference nonetheless: while in Thomas's time, commenting on this book was reserved to the bachelor's level, it became the essential work of the masters.

SUMMAS

With this last category we leave the world of orally transmitted teaching for that of the written form. We have now come to the point where we can correct the false notion, mentioned on the first page of this book: Thomas's *Summa* is neither the first nor the only one. In fact, the genre of "Summa" had been in existence since the twelfth century and can be found in all branches of learning. The term "Summa," even though somewhat vague, covers a variety of works: medicine, liturgy, exegesis, homiletics, law, theology, pastoral theology, and so forth. Toward 1272, a bookstore catalogue lists twenty titles of different kinds of Summas of which only three are properly speaking theological. Incidently, this helps us to understand why, even if it is permitted to use the abbreviated form "the *Summa*" in everyday language, it is better to avoid saying *"Summa theologica,"* for the adjective seems to subsume the substantive. Its proper name—found in all of the manuscripts—is *"Summa theologiae."*

According to P. Glorieux, the term "Summa" applies to three categories of work. The first is an encyclopedic work in a given field of study without much originality and which is sometimes referred to as a "compilation." Sometimes the word "compilation" can also be applied to *specula* ("mirrors") which, like that of Vincent of Beauvais, can be quite lengthy. Second, we also know of "shorter" Summas which, rather than being exhaustive, seek to summarize briefly and exactly the principle features. Finally, there are the "systematic" Summas, which are somewhere between an exhaustive compilation and a summary. They aim for an exact, complete, and especially organically structured presentation where nothing essential is missing.

Within the world of theology, it is clear that Thomas's work is to be found in the last category, but it is not without precedent. Among the most famous is the *Summa aurea* of William of Auxerre (around 1220), which, after the *Sentences* of Peter Lombard three-quarters of a century earlier, represents the first large-scale effort at this type of systematizing. As such, it will exercise some influence. Known by a fairly large public since the beginnings of printing, the *Summa aurea* has recently been published in a critical edition (J. Ribaillier, Paris-Grottaferrata, 1980–87). A little later, the *Summa de bono* of Philip the Chancellor remained in manuscript form for several centuries. It, too, has been published in a critical edition (N. Wicki, Bern, 1985). As significant as these two works are, they have neither the scope nor the originality of a work that followed them (it was finished in 1245) known under the title of *Summa fratris Alexandri* after the name of the Franciscan master, Alexander of Hales. He was the inspiration and brains behind the work, but not its sole contributor (Jean de la Rochelle and Odo Rigaud also had a hand in it; ed. Quaracchi, 1924–48). Nearer to Thomas is the *Summa de creaturis* of his master, Albert the Great (1245–48). We could also mention Albert's *Summa de mirabili scientia Dei,* which appeared at the end of his life (between 1270 and 1280) and was probably unknown to Thomas.

Further description of the literary landscape is unnecessary: we now know enough to understand the characteristics of Thomas's work better. With the Summas of a more systematic kind, Thomas's *Summa* strives to propose a synthetic doctrine. With the disputed questions, it shares a statement of the problem that allows for a reasoned progression and reserves within each treatise a strong interest for a *pro et contra* style of argumentation. For the educated reader, it is even exciting to discover, underneath each of the difficulties raised and the responses to them, as many valid objections coming from conflicting points of view, past or contemporaneous, or, on the contrary, echoes of the teaching of Scripture, the Fathers of the Church, and the most diverse philosophies. It is here, so as not to remain on the sidelines, that literary analysis must give way to a look at the sources.

The Christian Sources

We cannot examine all of the sources used in the writing of the *Summa,* for to do so would take us beyond the scope of this little book. More modestly, I would like to highlight two things: the scope of the information (we would not be mistaken in saying that Thomas read everything that he had at his disposal) and, more importantly, the intellectual and spiritual attitude that this denotes. The man who has been presented as a preeminent speculative genius, and who was no doubt that, was not an a priori thinker. On the contrary, he drew from all of the authors that he could lay his hands on.

THE BIBLE

In the first place, Sacred Scripture intimately penetrates Thomas's work. When he is referred to as a master of biblical sciences, we tend to think of his commentaries on several books of the Old Testament (Isaiah, Jeremiah, the Lamentations, Job, the Psalms) and most of the New Testament (Matthew, John, and all of St. Paul). But it would be a mistake to see these as an isolated part of his work. In truth, his other works are equally full of biblical references, and the *Summa* is no exception.

Statistics do not tell us everything, but they are useful. Since careful and patient scholars have already done the work, we will be pardoned if we use their numbers. Martin Hubert counted some 38,000 explicit citations in the *Summa theologiae* and the *Summa contra Gentiles.* Of this number, 25,000 come from the Bible, almost two-thirds. In a shorter opuscule (on the *Ten Commandments*, which is no longer than thirty-eight pages of one of our modern-day books of ordinary size), we find 491 citations, roughly 14 per page.

In addition to these numbers, we have to realize that for Thomas, the Bible is the Word of God in which he finds both his inspiration and his norm. It was a philosopher, Etienne

Gilson who expressed a profound, even though a bit exaggerated, truth: "For Thomas all of theology was a commentary on Scripture; he drew no conclusion without justifying it by some word of Sacred Scripture, which is the Word of God." We could easily produce here a series of convergent texts in support of this judgment. For the sake of illustration, let us cite what is perhaps the most categoric: "When it comes to the things of God, man should not easily speak of them otherwise than does Sacred Scripture" (*Contra errores graecorum* I, 1). Given that he held such principles, it is easy to see why Thomas's exegesis favors the literal meaning of the holy books. Even if his literal sense has little in common with the philological literalness favored by our contemporaries (since it includes the spiritual sense), it is certain that he sticks as closely as possible to the text.

As for the familiarity and the affection with which Thomas holds certain books, only more careful studies would be able to establish this with precision. But it seems that we can say that, of the Old Testament, Isaiah and the Wisdom literature are among his favorites. As for the New Testament, it would be difficult to decide between St. Paul and St. John. When it comes to the Christo-forming character of grace, the connection with St. Paul is clear: Thomas merely states in theological language what he finds in the Pauline epistles. The same thing can be said for the theme of the imitation of Christ, the theology of the Holy Spirit, and the relationship between law and grace. But we cannot say that the fourth gospel is absent when it comes to the Holy Spirit or the imitation of Christ. On the contrary, and as one would expect, John provides Thomas with much material concerning Christology and Trinitarian theology.

THE FATHERS

After the Scriptures in order of importance come those who commented on them, the Fathers of the Church or the *sancti* as Thomas called them: "We must retain not only what has been transmitted to us in the Scripture, but also the explanations of the holy doctors who preserved them for us intact" (*On the Divine Names* II, 1).

To return to the numbers that we have already used: of the 38,000 citations found in the two *Summas*, 8,000 come from Christian authors. We should also point out that we find 5,000 citations from pagan authors of which 4,300 are from the Philosopher, namely, Aristotle. This last figure is certainly not negligible, but we can see that it is not the only one. We should not overemphasize Aristotle's contribution to such an extent as to push into the background other sources that, statistically and doctrinally, are even more important.

If we seek to identify who these sources are, we should, of course, expect to find that the vast majority are Latin authors: Ambrose of Milan, Anselm of Canterbury, Bernard of Clairvaux, Gregory the Great, Jerome, Hilary of Poitiers, to mention the most cited. But Saint Augustine far outweighs them all. In the *Summa theologiae* alone, we find 2,000 citations from the Bishop of Hippo. According to a felicitous expression of L. Elders, the *Summa* was written in an "uninterrupted dialogue" with Augustine. Once and a while, Thomas discreetly disagrees with him, but for the most part he happily follows his lead. This means that we should seriously revise the perspective in which we speak of the "opposition" between the Augustinians and the Aristotelians, for a long time considered one of the historical keys to the thirteenth century.

In Thomas's work, the presence of the Greek tradition is no less important than that of the Latin tradition. The Gloss on the Bible had already transmitted a lot of patristic material, but two additional factors contributed decisively to expanding Thomas's knowledge. The writing of the *Golden Chain (Catena aurea)* caused important research to be done which provided Thomas with florilegia of Greek origin and of authors not then known (fifty-seven Greek authors are mentioned in the *Catena*). Moreover, the fact that he got to know the complete collection of the first councils contributed decisively to forming his Christological and Trinitarian thought. For example, the doctrine of the full humanity of Christ as an instrument *(organon)* of his divinity came directly from the Alexandrian fathers Athanasius and Cyril. But Thomas also received a lot from Maximus the Confessor by means of John Damascene concerning, for example, the doctrine of free will. It should not be surprising that he knew and quotes liberally from Origen, Basil the Great, John Chrysostom especially, and still more Pseudo-Dionysius the Areopagite. While none of these sources attains materially the importance of Augustine, the influence of Dionysius is no less profound.

We should add to this list an entire series of names cited less frequently. In keeping with the customs of the time which hesitated to mention the names of one's contemporaries, we never find the names of Albert or Bonaventure whom, as we know, Thomas followed closely. Others, a little further in the past, such as William of Auxerre, Prévostin of Cremona, Hugh and Richard of St. Victor, the Venerable Bede, and still others could usefully fill in this tableau. These sources, even if sporadically used, show by their diversity not only that Thomas is the faithful heir to the undivided Church, but that he is a scholar concerned with documentation and that he does not hesitate to use authors often less adept than he is.

Greeks, Jews, and Arabs

We are beginning to understand a bit better what Thomas owed to non-Christian thinkers, although work in this area is still in progress. Lacking a global or exhaustive evaluation, we nevertheless have a relatively precise idea concerning certain of these sources.

ARISTOTLE

The presence and influence of Aristotle in Thomas's writings no longer have to be shown. The author of choice of the young bachelor student continued to be so for the more mature man. Recent research confirms this prominence but also calls for some nuancing. Thomas is not the hard and fast Aristotelian that triomphalist Neothomists of the early half of the twentieth century like to imagine.

Thomas's adversaries began calling into question his faithfulness to Aristotle shortly after his death. His disciples had to concede quickly that he had somewhat gone beyond Aristotle's theories in an area as sensitive as the scientific quality of theology. If, at the beginning of the twentieth century, certain scholars delighted in seeing in him a faithful and careful exegete of Aristotle's works, others were quick to point out that Thomas did not hesitate to depart from Aristotle when he deemed it necessary. It is this second opinion that has won out and it is striking to notice that the positions have evolved toward more and more reserved judgments, but also more exact ones.

While recognizing that Thomas's exegesis is profound and

original, it must be said that he departed from Aristotle on some decisive points. The commentary on the *Ethics* is driven by the explicitly Christian principle of the beatific vision. The commentary on the *Metaphysics* is oriented toward a metaphysics of being completely foreign to Aristotle. Likewise, his theology of creation and his belief in the beginning of the world in time owe nothing to Aristotle, to say nothing of polytheism, about which a Christian theologian would not even dream.

It is true that Thomas retained so many important elements of Aristotle's thought that they cannot be numbered. Even reworked, the Aristotelian ideal of science remains a guiding principle for him, and, like all of his contemporaries, Thomas received from Aristotle a hierarchical conception of knowledge as well as the instruments of logical and metaphysical analysis without which his synthesis would have been unthinkable. It is sufficient to think of the fundamental categories of matter and form, potency and act, substance and accident, to understand that these are not tangential matters. If hylomorphism and the notion of the soul as the unique form of the human being or the theories of friendship and of happiness through contemplation take on a specifically Christian form in Thomas's writings, it is nonetheless to Aristotle that he owes them. What is more, from the number of models and beliefs that Thomas adopted, it can be said that what Aristotle gave him was a certain way of looking at the real. In fact, we recognize today that it was not the exact historical reconstitution of Aristotle's thought that interested Thomas. The concern of modern historians was not his own. Rather, he sought with Aristotle the truth, and this is why he did not hesitate to expand his perspectives, believing that in doing so he was being faithful to him.

MEDIEVAL NEOPLATONISM

The influence of Plato and Plotinus in the Middle Ages is a different story from that of Aristotle. While the progressive diffusion of translations of Aristotle allowed medieval scholars almost complete access to his works from the middle of the thirteenth century on, the same cannot be said for Plato, of whom they possessed only three works (*Timaeus, Meno, Phaedo,* the last were little known), or for Plotinus whose works had not been translated. Medieval Platonism (where it is difficult to distinguish between Platonism and Neoplatonism) is nonetheless an important reality due to a number of works that had passed down their ideas. In the first place, we have Augustine and Pseudo-Dionysius, but also Boethius, Macrobius, Martianus Capella, Avicenna, *the Liber de causis,* and several works of Proclus. Through them it was inevitable that a certain number of "Platonic" elements found their way into the *Summa* and other works of Thomas's.

Even if we were only to retain Augustine, there would already be too much to say to confine ourselves to what came from him. Let us be satisfied with simply recalling Thomas's important debt to him for his Christian transposition of the Platonic notion of Ideas in the form of eternal reasons present in the divine understanding in which all created realities participate. If this participation comes about by means of a free creation and not by emanation, it nonetheless presupposes a divine exemplarism that is, in fact, at work in Master Thomas.

Even though Dionysius's influence is less felt than that of Augustine's, it is still considerable. We can find 1,702 explicit citations in Thomas's work of which 562 are in the *Summa.* To believe the specialists: if we were to count the implicit citations, we would have to double that figure. We also know that more than half of these citations come from the *Divine Names* and this is why we find them especially in Thomas's doctrine of God. In fact, Dionysius introduced into Christian theology the theory of the three ways (causality, negation, eminence) leading to the knowledge of God. But Thomas does not follow him unhesitatingly in his apophatism (from the Greek *apophasis:* negation; a word sometimes used as the equivalent of "negative theology," which is Pseudo-Dionysius's own term). For Thomas, the negative moment is but a stage in the complex path that leads to an analogical but nonetheless real knowledge of God.

The Neoplatonic influence, through Dionysius, can be seen again in the hierarchical vision of the universe dear to Thomas and probably also in the circular structure of the *Summa.* Dionysius is also present in other areas as well, such as angelology, Christology, and the sacraments (in the category of sign for sacraments in general and in baptismal illumination in particular). This influence is nonetheless carefully filtered at certain decisive points: for Thomas God is not beyond being, as Dionysius insisted, but is on the contrary subsistent Being itself *(ipsum esse subsistens).* Again contrary to Dionysius, being has primacy over the good for Thomas, and it is in an Aristotelian sense that he interprets the famous axiom "goodness tends to be diffusive of itself" [*bonum est diffusivum sui*].

As brief as they are, these reflections allow us to understand better the ways by which Neoplatonism counterbalanced the influence of Aristotle. I could mention other examples in the area of noetics and ontology. But for certain elements that could have their origin in Plato, we should probably not completely put aside the theory that they may have come by way of Aristotle himself, who remained more Platonic than commonly believed. We need not pursue these investigations any further. It is enough to have begun to show the rich diversity of the soil in which the *Summa* is rooted.

THE STOICS

Stoicism is a current of thought that is also widely present in the *Summa*. According to the specialists, no ancient movement has been so carefully analyzed by Thomas as this one. Still, with the exception of Seneca, Thomas had no direct access to Stoic works. The indirect sources are numerous, however, and convey to him the essential ideas: Boethius and Macrobius, Nemesius of Emesa (under the name of Gregory of Nyssa), Ambrose and Augustine, but especially Cicero, whose Stoic tendencies were not unknown.

The vast majority of these references to the *Stoici* are found in the moral part of the work. Thus, of the 300 citations from Cicero that Clement Vansteenkiste found in the entire work, 168 are in the Second Part (48 in Ia IIae; 120 in IIa IIae). As M. Spanneut underscored, this influence is especially evident in two major areas: that of virtue and the virtues and that of the moral and the natural law. A connection is made between the two by the idea of nature itself, since to live according to nature is to live according to reason and virtue (see Ia IIae q. 18, a. 5), for the natural law is a participation of the eternal law in rational creatures. For his part, Thomas introduces a fair number of precisions and refinements, but all of the essential points of his doctrine have corresponding elements in the Stoic masters.

As for virtue, it is also well established that Thomas borrowed from Cicero the general structure of his teaching on the moral virtues, with the four cardinal virtues and the sixteen virtues connected to them, which constitutes the structure of a large part of the *Summa*. More often than not, Thomas respects the order and the definitions proposed by Cicero such that, through him, this way of speaking of the virtues remained common coin for Christian morality. But if we wish to appreciate exactly where he situates himself in all of this, it has to be added that Thomas knows how to keep his distance and constantly rejects Stoic absolutism. It is a mistake, he says, to say that the wise man is never sad, and it is not reasonable to pretend that the virtuous are always happy (see Ia IIae q. 59 a. 3). We should not forget either that, in spite of the formal connections, the intervention of grace radically changes the content of this edifice, since it raises it to a level that is no longer that of pure nature.

AVICENNA

More perhaps than on Aristotle, the Neoplatonists, and the Stoics, recent research has focused on Arab-speaking thinkers. For the sake of simplicity, we will concentrate on the three most important: Avicenna, Averroës, and Maimonides. It has long been established that Thomas was familiar with them, but because of a lack of sufficient research, we had to limit ourselves to vague generalities. Over the course of the twentieth century, this situation has changed, and we have come to realize the immense contribution of Arab culture to the West in general and, more precisely, to the areas of philosophy and theology. Before reviewing each of the thinkers, it should be noted that they do not stand alongside the Greek thinkers as simply other independent sources. Certain Greek works are known to the West only through their Arab intermediaries, and they themselves are connected to one or another of the currents of ancient Greek thought.

The major writings of the earliest among them, Avicenna (980–1037), a philosopher and doctor, could be read in a Latin translation from the second half of the twelfth century *(Canon on Medicine and Metaphysics)*. First received favorably, he was later criticized by William of Auvergne in 1230, but remained in favor among certain English Franciscans such as Roger Bacon and Duns Scotus. As for Thomas, he cites him about 450 times. Avicenna's influence is quite strong in the treatise *De ente et essentia* (before 1256), and if Thomas cites him numerous times in the *Sentences* (more than 150 times in the first two books), in the two series of disputed questions *De veritate* and *De potentia,* and in several other older works, he becomes more rare as time goes on, eventually disappearing almost entirely.

Now we have to point out a curious phenomenon: if the name of Avicenna disappears, his teaching is still recognizable in a number of places, and so we have to ask the reasons for this silence. The most likely reason, perhaps, would be that Thomas did not want to compromise a teaching that he deemed to be true with the name of a philosopher who was more and more under attack. George Anawati established a list of forty-seven instances of ideas, definitions, and distinctions from Avicenna approved by Thomas. But he also emphasizes the fact that Thomas distances himself from him on decisive matters such as the existence of secondary causes, the theory of the separated agent intellect, the necessity of creation, the creation from all eternity, the denial of free will and of the resurrection of the body, and so on. Most importantly, we might add, Thomas's philosophy is before all else that of existent being, whereas Avicennism is a form of essentialism. In spite of the multiplicity of things that Thomas borrowed from Avicenna, we cannot qualify his synthesis as Avicennian.

AVERROËS

What was said of Avicenna must also be said of Averroës (1126–98), whose writings did not become part of the intellectual world until Michael Scotus's translation in around 1230. According to C. Vansteenkiste (who also counted Aquinas's use of Avicenna), Thomas cites Averroës 500 times in his writings but especially in his philosophical works, given that this Arab thinker was then seen as the commentator on Aristotle par excellence. Certain disparities are nonetheless striking. While we find 177 references to Averroës in the *Sentences,* often in approval of him or which interpret his questionable positions favorably, we find a mere 21 in the *Summa.*

The evolution of Aquinas's use of Averroës is therefore parallel to that of Avicenna. Still, even when Thomas diverges from Avicenna he always refers to him with respect while, in the case of Averroës, we find with time a growing number of disagreements and even out-and-out rejection. The strongest of these are found in the Question *On the Unity of the Intellect* where he is no longer called a "commentator" but a "corrupter" of Aristotle's thought *(depravator* or *perversor).*

If Thomas's references to Averroës indicate Thomas's knowledge of him, this does not mean that he was influenced by him blindly. Thus when it comes to the questions on the relationship between philosophy and theology or on the unity of the intellect for all men, we find Thomas engaged in a frontal attack. But without a doubt, in the area of natural philosophy, Thomas received from Averroës his notions of infinity, of time, of numbers, of movement, and of matter. Thomas also makes frequent use of his axioms like "every agent acts according to what he is" [*omne agens agit simile sibi*], or concerning the definition of *habitus* as "that by which we can act as we wish" [*habitus est quo quis agit cum voluerit*]. Likewise, he often cites favorably Averroës' maxim concerning the importance of the moral virtues in the exercise of the speculative sciences.

MAIMONIDES

The question of the presence of Maimonides (1135–1204), an Arabic-speaking Jewish thinker, in the writings of Thomas is not entirely new. We have known for a long time that Aquinas refers to his *Guide of the Perplexed* when speaking of the obstacles to the natural knowledge of God, of the theory of prophecy, or of the value of the ceremonial precepts of the Old Law. But the recent research of Ruedi Imbach has allowed us to be more precise about these general statements. Just as with Avicenna and just as curiously, Thomas clearly makes use of Maimonides for the demonstration of the existence of God (in the third way) or when discussing the eternity of the world, yet does not cite him. On the contrary, with respect to the divine names, to the divine knowledge of particulars, to Providence, and to the nature and number of separated substances, he discusses his position as that of an adversary. This presence of the Jewish thinker, found only in the area of theology, is modest but consistent (82 references in all of Thomas's work; 18 in the *Summa*). If we consider that, at the time when Thomas was beginning to teach, Latin translations of Maïmonides' work were still recent, we have here a new indication of his attention to the contemporary movement of ideas. We would have another example were we to consider Thomas's relations with the Faculty of Arts where he was much more appreciated than at the Faculty of Theology. But that is a topic for another time.

While space does not allow us to explore all of the questions raised by these sources, there is one that we cannot avoid. After setting forth all of these sources and their numerous tributaries, we might be tempted to wonder what is properly Aquinas's. As for the implicit citations, we have to acknowledge that all medieval writers did this. Copyright laws were not perceived as they are now. Many ideas were considered to be public property, and no one felt the need to reference his sources. Thomas's strength lies in the fact the he did not simply create a mosaic of all of these sources. What he wrote was his own; his teaching was not mere eclecticism, but an original synthesis. We can apply to theology a saying of Gilson: "a philosophy must not be defined by the elements it borrows, but by the spirit that animates it." If we agree with this, we will see in Thomas's teaching neither Platonism nor Aristotelianism, not Avicennism and even less Averroïsm, but Christianity. As for the features proper to his thought, the attacks that were subsequently made on them brought them clearly to the fore.

The *Summa* through History

IF THOMAS'S LIFE WAS RELATIVELY EVENTFUL, the reception
of his doctrine was positively tumultuous. Without reviewing here the entire history of Thomism, it is important to
recall its major moments, for it is not always possible to isolate
from them those things that concern the *Summa* in particular,
and it is certain that it was around the synthetically organized
doctrine of this work that opposition and openness were crystal-
lized. For more than two centuries, university professors no
doubt continued to comment on the *Sentences,* but the *Summa*
slowly made its way and assumed the place it would have in the
curriculum.

We usually distinguish three key moments in this history: the
first two centuries after Thomas's death in 1274, a period that
went from violent polemics to one of serenity; the flourishing of
classical and baroque scholasticism with the publication of important commentaries on the *Summa,* then recognized as a major work (1450–1800); a period of renewal in the nineteenth
century with Leo XIII's encyclical *Aeterni Patris,* during which
Thomism took on diverse forms. I will return to this renaissance
in the next chapter where, without knowing yet whether we
have entered into a new era, I will describe the current state of
affairs.

First Period (1274–1450)

Few documents are as well known among medievalists as the one dated March 7, 1277. Three years to the day after Thomas's death, Etienne Tempier, then the bishop of Paris, condemned a series of 219 propositions judged to be heterodox. This document, explicitly directed against certain opinions expressed at the Faculty of Arts, did not attack Thomas except indirectly. But Robert Wielockx has recently discovered that Thomas's doctrine was also the object of direct attacks. Transferred to Rome, the trial was stopped by cardinals friendly to the Order of Preachers. Thomas's canonization by Pope John XXII in 1323 made him untouchable, and a new bishop of Paris, Etienne Bourret, soon declared that the condemnation of his predecessor did not apply to Thomas (1325). This, however, did not put an end to the theological controversy.

FIRST POLEMICS

Even while he was living, certain points of Master Thomas's teaching provoked the concern of a confrere, the English Dominican Robert Kilwardby. Becoming Archbishop of Oxford in 1273, he condemned certain Thomistically inspired theses on March 18, 1277. His successor, the Franciscan John Pecham, an old adversary from Thomas's Paris days, renewed this condemnation ten years later.

The most forceful opposition came from another English Franciscan, William de la Mare who, around 1279, published a Catalogue *(Correctorium)* of 118 Thomistic theses deemed dangerous, attached to which were censures as well as criticisms and proposed corrections. He structured his Catalogue using annotations in the margins of the incriminating texts that were to be taught by masters and students. This work was thought to be so useful that the Franciscans, meeting in Strasbourg in 1282, decreed that its readers could only use the *Summa* if the corrections appeared with it.

What a superb historical witness to the power of a text! Less than ten years after finishing it, Master Thomas's work had achieved sufficient importance even among his adversaries that, in spite of not being able to stop its spread, they judged it necessary to reduce its effect. If not all of these theses came from the *Summa* (forty-two came from other writings of Thomas), it did provide the most significant amount, some seventy-six in all: forty-eight from the First Part, thirty-eight from the Second Part (the Third Part, not yet in circulation in Paris, was temporarily left uncensored).

The most famous of these theses concerned the manner in which God will be known in the beatific vision: without any created concept, but in his very essence. From his reading of Scripture, Thomas is certain that we will see God face-to-face with no intermediary (Ia q. 12 a. 2). In addition, Thomas asserts the following: God's knowledge of future contingents in the present of his eternity (Ia q. 14 a. 13); the beginning of the world in time, which Thomas believes is not demonstrable and which faith alone can affirm (Ia q. 46 a. 2); the hylomorphic composition (from the Greek *hylē:* matter and *morphē:* form) of angels and of the human soul (rather than speaking of matter and form with respect to them, Thomas safeguards the import of these clumsy expressions ["matter" is hardly appropriate for spirits] by replacing them with the composition of essence and existence, the first having to do with power and the second with act [see Ia q. 50 a. 2 and q. 75 a. 5]).

At issue in these theses is the question of the unicity of substantial form in man. While the Franciscans, following Bonaventure, accepted a plurality of forms (spiritual, sensitive, and vegetative) arranged hierarchically among themselves, Thomas believed that they are three functions of the one soul that is both simple and indivisible (Ia q. 76 a. 3). A seemingly abstract notion to the uninitiated, Thomas's positions had very real consequences for theology. In addition to these, Thomas held other divergent positions as well. These concern the theory of knowledge (to Augustine's theory of intellectual illumination Thomas prefers abstraction from the senses) and the primacy of the intellect over the will, which can be found in his concept of theology (speculative for Thomas, practical for Bonaventure), a concept that will divide theological discussion in the years ahead between the intellectualists and volontarists.

The Dominicans could not remain silent in the face of the attacks against someone who was already the glory of their Order. From 1277 until the eve of Thomas's canonization, the general chapters intervened regularly: first negatively, by suppressing the too violent attacks coming from outside the Order; then positively, by recommending the study of his doctrine. The renewal of these recommendations suggests that things were not as easy as they might appear. In fact, history has preserved the names of famous Dominican opponents of Thomas's thought. Some, like Durand of Saint-Pourçain, were strongly attacked for their ideas while others, like Thierry of Freiberg, could, so it seems, express themselves more freely.

Without spending too much time on this, I should point out that the dispute lasted for a long time and a lot of difficulties had to be overcome before Thomas was considered a theological "authority" outside of the Dominican order. A debate that arose at the University of Paris at the end of the fourteenth century witnesses eloquently to this. When, in 1387, the young Spanish theologian Juan de Montson tried to defend certain Thomistic theses (we need not enter into the details of them here), an accusation of heresy leveled against him was quickly transformed into a discussion and then a trial of the authority of Thomas. The Dominican masters took the side of their confrere by calling upon the Pope, and this was the occasion for the chancellor Pierre d'Ailly to present to the pontifical court a series of arguments that showed that Thomas was only one doctor among many, that he changed his positions during his career, that there were inconsistencies and errors in his work. Still debated, the doctrine of the unicity of substantial form was declared to be scandalous by Pierre d'Ailly. The propositions of Juan de Montson were condemned, and the Dominicans' refusal to accept this verdict saw them excluded from the University until 1403.

THE BEGINNINGS OF THOMISM

Just how faithful to Thomas his first disciples were is a complex question. The transition between the thirteenth and the fourteenth centuries is difficult to describe. It is enough to know that the *Corrections* of William de la Mare did not remain unanswered. Between 1280 and 1290 we can count no less than five of Thomas's confreres who undertook the task of refuting it (Richard Knapwell, John of Paris, and Rambert of Bologna are the most known). None of them is yet a master, which indicates that they were young and no doubt more sensitive to the novelty of their elder's theses. If we add to these names those of Thomas Sutton, Bernard de Trilia, Hervé of Nédellec, and Remi of Florence, we will have the most important names of those years.

Without forming a school in the proper sense of the word, these first disciples subscribed in general to a certain number of the major theses recalled above. In defense of their master, they put forward his own texts and were thus the first to use a method that would remain fruitful but which could not always avoid a sclerotic repetitiveness. At the same time, there appeared the first generation of anonymous exegetes who devoted themselves to highlighting the progress that Thomas had made between the writing of the *Sentences* and the *Summa*. Besides William de la Mare's attacks, this is the first sign that Thomas was being seen in his singularity. To these first working tools were added Tables and Concordances of Thomas's work of which the *Tabula aurea* of Peter of Bergamo (1473), which is still useful, was the crowning glory.

We can quickly pass over what follows. In the battle against Scotism and Ockhamism, the Thomism of this period became itself more quibbling and rigid. It will suffer indirectly from the ravages of the plague, the decadence of the Dominican order, and the Great Schism (1378–1417), which also divided the Dominicans. The renewal of the Order under Raymond of Capua (1380–99) will give it a new vitality, to which an increase in the number of masters of theology to supply the growing number of universities throughout Europe will attest (in truth, the growing number of masters is an ambiguous sign since many, out of vainglory, wanted to become masters). The translations of the *Summa* into Greek and Armenian and the knowledge that the humanist masters of the Italian Renaissance will have of it is also a sign of the interest that the *Summa* excited.

A little later, one of the most famous authors of this time, John Cabrol, better known under the name of Capreolus (1380–1444), wrote his *Defense of the Theology of Saint Thomas* (completed in 1432) within the framework of a commentary on the *Sentences*. This work, which was to have an enormous success (three complete editions in the course of a century and several abridged versions), witnesses its author's deep knowledge of the whole of Thomas's work. It has abundant citations and defends Thomas against a host of adversaries: Henry of Ghent, Duns Scotus, Gregory of Rimini, Durand of Saint-Pourçain, Peter Auriol. His knowledge of the first generation of Thomists and of the polemics of this period makes Capreolus a precious link for the masters of the sixteenth century (especially Cajetan). Even if they have a direct knowledge of certain works, it is from him that they derive most of their knowledge of this period. The reverse side of the coin is that his faithfulness brings with it a certain archaic quality: Capreolus, who knows the authors of the fourteenth century very well, seems to have no knowledge of his contemporaries.

Second Period (1450–1800)

Much research is still needed in order to have a more exact and complete idea of the state of Thomism in the second half of the fifteenth century. Even more reason that the precise object of our research should be the fate of the *Summa!* The diffusion of his text in manuscript or printed form thus constitutes an important piece of information.

THE ADVENT OF THE 'SUMMA'

At the present time we possess between two hundred and three hundred manuscripts of the *Summa*. Their number varies according to the Parts for they were reproduced separately (246 for the *Prima;* 220 for the *Prima Secundae;* 280 for the *Secunda Secundae;* 213 for the *Tertia*). These numbers do not reflect the actual situation before the invention of the printing press. At that time many manuscripts were lost, as they were deemed to be useless. Others disappeared as a consequence of natural disasters or war (floods, fires, and bombings). Still others became unusable because of natural disintegration and the like. According to "optimistic" estimates from an expert as well versed in the area as L.-J. Bataillon, we have today only about a tenth of the manuscripts that transmitted the text of the *Summa.* According to him, to speak of two or three thousand copies would still be an underestimation. Compared to the size of the literate world at the time, this number still means a considerable diffusion of Thomas's work.

The invention of the printing press was to bring a new and decisive expansion to this diffusion. If we were to consider the early printed books conserved in the National Library of France alone, we know that before the end of the fifteenth century, twenty-nine printed editions of the *Summa,* either in part or entire, had already been published (the total number could surpass forty). In Italy alone seventeen were published, twelve in Venice (an important center of early printing) in less than twenty years. The oldest of these editions seems to be that of the *Prima Secundae* in Strasbourg before 1463, followed shortly thereafter by the *Secunda Secundae* at Mayence in 1467, then in Bale before 1474, while the *Prima* appeared in Cologne around 1468 and the *Tertia* in Bale around 1474. The interests of the scholars who took the initiative to publish these texts explains the haphazard order of publication. But the three Parts of the *Summa* were also edited simultaneously: in Bale in 1485, in Venice in 1495, and in Nuremberg in 1496. Italy and the Rhine countries were favored; no work of Thomas's was printed in Paris during the fifteenth century. We have to wait until 1512 to see the *Secunda Secundae* published at the request of Pierre Crockaert, who entrusted it to his most famous student, Francisco de Vitoria. One year later, in 1513, the *Prima Secundae* will be published by Antoine Coronel, the regent of the Sorbonne.

This extraordinary burgeoning of the early printed editions of the *Summa* is, in and of itself, indicative of the reading habits of the time. Editors then, no less than today, would not have marketed books for the sole pleasure of seeing them go unsold. There was, in fact, a definite demand. The basic book for university teaching was not the *Summa* but the *Sentences.* Still, in spite of the invention of the printing press, these first editions are not the fruit of spontaneous generation. Rather, they were the fruit of the oral teaching that preceded them.

From the beginning of the fourteenth century, some Dominicans from the province of Rome dared to use the *Summa* as the basis of their teaching. For this they were reprimanded by the chapter of Perugia in 1308, which ordered them to stick to the *Sentences.* One year later, in 1309, even if the general chapter of Saragossa charged the Dominican "lecturers" to teach according to the doctrine and work of Thomas, the presumed basic text was still to be the *Sentences.* This was confirmed by the general chapter of Metz in 1313, but John of Sterngassen, whose teaching on the *Sentences* can be dated to around 1320, often appealed to the *Summa* for his commentary on Lombard, giving an example of the way in which one could combine the doctrinal recommendations with the practice of producing a commentary. At the same time, and at the request of John XXII who canonized Thomas, Giovanni Dominici wrote a summary of the *Summa* in which we can rightly see a precursor to the future great commentaries. But we must also mention the summaries of the *Secunda Secundae* (the most useful Part for confessors!) that we owe to various authors who circulated, not without a certain impoverishment, Thomas's teaching on moral matters.

If we remember that, in the days following the death of Thomas, it was the work of Albert the Great that was being taught at Cologne, it is rather surprising to see that the practice of commenting on the *Summa* rather than on the *Sentences* appeared in this city. If the recommendation to study the whole of Thomas's work appeared in the Dominican *studia* beginning in 1424, and if this practice was encouraged at Cologne in 1483 by the Master of the Order, Salvo Casetta, the one who gave the impetus for this was the secular priest Henry of Gorcum (d. 1431), who not only taught using the *Summa,* but also wrote a *Compendium of the Summa* (which would be printed in 1473). It was thus that he was able to move Thomas's work from a secondary place at the University to a primary one. The decisive step seems to have been taken by Johannes Tinctor (d. 1469), who publicly commented on the *Prima* and the *Prima Secundae* at the University. He was followed shortly thereafter by Gerhard von Elten (d. 1484), who also commented on the text of the First Part. As for Laurent Gervais (d. 1483), he follows step-by-step the entire *Summa* in his *Declarationes articulorum Summae s. Thomae.* Still, the most remarkable of these masters was Conrad Köllin, first a professor at Heidelberg (1507–11), then at Cologne (1511–36), to whom we owe both an explanation, until then unedited, of the First Part and, more importantly, the first published commentary on the *Prima Secundae* (1512).

From Cologne, this practice extended to a number of universities of the Germanic world: Vienna, with a student of Tinctor, L. Huntpichler (from 1443); Fribourg, with Caspar Grünwald (in 1490); Rostock, with Kornelius van Sneek and Johannes Hoppe. It was only slightly later that the practice spread elsewhere: Cajetan, after having "read" the *Sentences* at Padua, taught using the *Summa* at Pavia from 1497 to 1499 and soon published his great commentary, beginning with the *Prima Pars*.

At Paris, we know that Gilles Charronelle, a Dominican, had, in 1508, already taught Thomism for twenty years. His student, Pierre Crockaert, at first a nominalist, converted to Thomism after entering the Domincans at Saint-Jacques, and taught the *Summa* from 1509 onwards. In 1523, the general chapter of Valladolid probably echoed this practice when it ordered Saint-Jacques to teach three lessons per day from Saint Thomas *(tres lectiones quotidie de sancto Thoma)* to the students sent from other houses to study there. On the other hand, at the University of Louvain we will have to wait until 1596 for the *Summa* to replace the *Sentences* in its curriculum. By this time, the tradition of commentaries and of commentators had already won acclaim.

CAJETAN

Thomas de Vio, better known as Cajetan (from *Gaetano,* that is, from Gaeta: 1465–1534) has been, without doubt, the best-known exegete of Thomas ever since Pope Pius V ordered him to publish his explanation of the *Summa* with the first complete edition of the works of Master Thomas. This edition, which we call the *Piana* (from the name of the pope; Rome, 1570), is still used. But it is used less than two other more recent editions: *Parma* (from its place of origin; 1852–73) and *Vivès* (after the name of the printer; Paris, 1871–72). These two latest editions do not reproduce Cajetan's text, which is found in the Leonine edition (from Pope Leo XIII) and about which we will speak later. The practice of combining the text of Cajetan with Thomas's no doubt contributed to its diffusion. But Cajetan himself can hardly be ignored. After receiving his Master's degree in Theology by virtue of a brilliant debate with Pico della Mirandola (1494), he first taught the *Sentences* at Padua before going on to Pavia (1497–99) to teach the *Summa*. He was the first to do so in Italy and his commentary—published over the period from 1507 to 1522, as he was already the Master of the Dominican order, a bishop, and a cardinal—was also the first to be a complete commentary and was, as a whole, quite remarkable.

As in the case of so many works on the *Sentences,* the title of "commentary" can be deceiving. Cajetan is a thinker of great scope and innovation who, under the guise of explaining the text, often introduces changes of terms and content. According to Etienne Gilson, his essentialization of the Thomistic concept of being would have necessarily led him to renounce the rational demonstration of the immortality of the soul. He also has his own positions on the doctrine of analogy, on the formal component of the personality, on original justice, on the sacrifice of the Mass, and on the causality of the sacraments. His philosophical positions also have repercussions in theology, as can be seen in his interpretation of the natural desire to see God for which he elaborates a theory of obediential power that is quite far from what we find in Thomas.

In other areas though, we do find in Cajetan an authentic

Thomistic methodology. Cajetan is an eager biblical exegete, and in this he takes positions that are truly audacious in order to confront the arguments of the reformers (he was Leo X's legate and met Luther in 1518). This earned him praise on the one hand and censure from the Sorbonne on the other, as well as the uninformed criticism of some of his confreres. As a moralist, he followed his profound commentary of the Secunda Pars with a *Little Summa of Sins* for use by confessors, in which he treats in alphabetical order contemporary problems of pastoral care including economic and social questions. This little treatise on sin is not nearly as sophisticated as his biblical exegesis, for in it he revives a tradition that was no doubt longstanding in the Order, but which Thomas deliberately wanted to go beyond. In spite of the renown that Cajetan enjoyed, we should not see him as the sole authentic interpreter of Thomas. If his position as the Master of the Order inhibited his critics from being too vocal, the opposition that his theological ideas met on the part of his contemporaries (Sylvester of Prierio and Sylvester of Ferrara most notably, the latter being the renowned commentator of the *Summa contra Gentiles*) could not be silenced.

VITORIA AND THE SCHOOL OF SALAMANCA

The "golden age" of Spain was so called for several reasons. In its extraordinary theological burgeoning, Thomism also had its place due to two famous centers of study: Valladolid for philosophy and Salamanca for theology. Leaving the first aside, let us focus on the second where Francisco de Vitoria had established the practice of commenting on the *Summa* in ground already prepared by Diego de Deza (d. 1523), who had introduced Thomism there. Sent to Paris to complete his studies (1508–13),

Vitoria benefited from the instruction of Jean du Feynier, who would later become the successor of Cajetan as the Master of the Dominican order, and of Pierre Crockaert. The latter entrusted him with the task of publishing the *Secunda Secundae,* the first published edition of the *Summa* in Paris (1512). It is important to note that in the preface, Vitoria underscores two of Thomas's qualities that would make him acceptable to the humanists of the time: his frequent citing from Holy Scripture and his abundant recourse to the Latin and Greek thinkers of antiquity.

Upon his return to Salamanca, Vitoria taught from 1523 until his death in 1545, forming a group of disciples around him. He had, as an occasional substitute then colleague, Dominic Soto (1494–1560), who replaced him at the Council of Trent. Vitoria's successor in 1546, Melchior Cano (1509–60), would become one of the most famous representatives of this school, among whose members we should mention Dominic Bañez (1528–1604), councilor to and defender of Saint Teresa of Avila, to whom the Carmelite reform owed much. Besides being commentators of the *Summa,* all of these theologians share a common concern for scriptural and patristic sources, a concern that was very much Thomas's own.

In differing degrees, these theologians also shared a concern for political ethics because of the colonization of the New World. But Vitoria surpassed all of them by the quality and courage of his interventions. In 1537, in the context of his commentary on the *Secunda Secundae,* his course *On Temperance,* which was the occasion for an attack on colonial policies toward the indigenous populations, earned him a letter of rebuke by Emperor Charles V, sent to the Prior of his convent. Two years later, in 1539, he presented two famous "lessons," *On the Indians* and *On the Right of War,* rightly considered to be the foundations of modern international law. Thereafter, he would be the representative of imperial power on these questions, and the new laws regarding the Indies that were passed in 1542 bear the marks of his ideas concerning the rights of indigenous populations.

As moving as he was in denouncing abuses (which he knew firsthand from his missionary confreres), Vitoria remained a theologian capable of tight rational argumentation indebted to a tradition that went back to Saint Thomas (he also cites Cajetan in his commentary on IIa IIae q. 68 a. 8). If Vitoria is of interest to us because of the fruitfulness of Thomas's doctrine, it is because he does not see the natural law that he stresses as a voluntary creation, such as is the case with positive law. Rather, for him the natural law is founded on the very nature of man himself: a person created free in the image of God and made for living with others. This is why the Indians must be respected as persons and as peoples in the institutions that they have made for themselves. One cannot make war against them because they refuse the true faith, for only a grave injustice can provide the grounds for a war if it is to be just. If someone were convinced of the injustice of war, he would not be permitted to engage in it even if the king ordered it.

Quickly printed and sent throughout all of Europe, the texts of Vitoria had an influence that went beyond the tragic episode that impelled him to write them. It would take too long to list all of the Catholic theologians that were indebted to him either directly or through his students, but we should at least mention the famous Protestant jurist Hugo Grotius (1583–1645), nick-named the "father of the rights of man" who, in his writings, especially the *De jure belli ac pacis (On the Right of War and Peace),* often quotes from the writings of Vitoria and his disciples. Through them, he comes into contact with Saint Thomas, the "theologian of the true religion," who taught that "the purpose of war is to banish or to make disappear all that troubles the peace" (cf. IIa IIae q. 40 a.1 ad 3).

JOHN OF ST. THOMAS

Even though he was not as famous as Vitoria, John Poinsot, better known under his religious name John of St. Thomas (1589–1644), is still one of the great representatives of the diffusion of Thomas's thought. Viennese on his father's side and Portuguese on his mother's, he pursued his studies at Coimbra and then at Louvain, before taking the Dominican habit in Spain. He taught first at the Dominican college and then at the University of Alcalá for a total of thirty years before becoming the confessor of Philip IV of Spain.

Unlike Cajetan and Vitoria who wrote detailed commentaries on Thomas's work, John of St. Thomas used it as a springboard to enter more fully into the great debates of his time. The era of the great commentators had come to an end; John of St. Thomas began that of the *disputationes* (the same method was used a century later by the Carmelites of Salamanca). An emblematic figure of Neothomism like Cajetan, John of St. Thomas has become more recently, also like him, a sign of contradiction. Cornelio Fabro asserts that in order to rediscover the source of Thomism, we have to study the commentators in the reverse direction of the route they would seem to indicate. Jacques Maritain, albeit an admirer of John of St. Thomas, does not hesitate to denounce his "typically Baroque-scholastic complications," the shortsightedness of his petty polemics, and his lack of attention to the renewal of science in his own time.

In fact, we must, like Maritain, recognize in the work of John of St. Thomas numerous shortcomings that are at the origin of the discredit into which the Thomism of the twentieth century fell. With no concern for history, John of St. Thomas was acquainted only with the most recent scholastic authors such as Suarez and Vasquez with whom he readily disagreed. Lacking any regard for internal criticism, he does not hesitate to affirm that Thomas would not have been opposed to the Immaculate Conception of the Virgin Mary. Moreover, he locates the formal component of the divine essence in the *intelligere subsistens* (the actual intellection of God by himself), thus demonstrating that he had not grasped the power of Thomas's *ipsum esse subsistens* (subsistent Being itself).

According to an expression often used after him, John of St. Thomas holds that the true disciple is not content merely to follow Master Thomas; rather, he extends his thinking. His personal positions are thus numerous, intentionally so. In the area of the theory of knowledge and of the life of the mind (sign, agent intellect, concept, love, knowledge by connaturality), they are sometimes even fortunate. Concerning the nature of theology, he has great concern for synthetic unity. But while Thomas focused before all else on the internal organization of the deposit of revelation ("ostensive" theology), John of St. Thomas was one of the first to situate the object of theology in the deduction of new conclusions, thereby inaugurating a shift that was harmful both for the understanding and for the practice of theology. To his credit, John of St. Thomas gave great attention to Thomas's theology of the Holy Spirit. He is the author of a beautiful treatise on the gifts of the Holy Spirit that was rediscovered in the twentieth century (thanks to a translation by Raïssa Maritain). As in the case of Capreolus, John of St. Thomas's genius and his place in history guarantee him a preeminent position in spreading Thomas's work. He is the immediate source of the influential works of J.-B. Gonnet (d. 1681), A. Goudin (d. 1695), V. L. Gotti (d. 1742) and Ch.-R. Billuart (d. 1757).

THE JESUITS AND THE CARMELITES

By the time of John of St. Thomas, Thomism was no longer the exclusive domain of the Dominicans. Other religious orders, notably the Carmelites and the Jesuits, had adopted it more or less officially. According to their founder's wishes, the Jesuits were to study and teach using the *Summa* of Saint Thomas. This is precisely what Francisco Toledo (1533–96), a theologian of the first generation, did. But Saint Ignatius himself and even more so his successors wanted a new theology capable of reconciling Thomists, Scotists, and nominalists. This eclecticism found its most eminent representatives in the persons of Francis Suarez (1548–1617) and Gabriel Vasquez (1549–1604), both of whom left important commentaries on the *Summa* in the line of Vitoria and Cano as to method and attention to sources. If Vasquez was more of a Molinist than a Thomist in his doctrine of grace, Suarez had, among his other merits, that of being attentive in his commentary on the *Tertia Pars* to the mysteries of the life of Christ, generally neglected by other Thomists.

As for the Carmelites, they are at the origin of a collective work that is made up of two courses: one philosophical, known as the *Complutenses* (7 volumes, published at Acalà beginning in 1624); the other theological, known as the *Salmanticenses* (10 vol-

umes, published anonymously at Salamanca, from 1600 to 1725).
Hailed originally and for a long time as monuments of fidelity
to Master Thomas, these works can be characterized more precisely as reflections of the Thomism of the time. Their lack of
sensitivity to history, already seen in John of St. Thomas, caused
them to neglect the sources and to omit certain treatises (for example, the mysteries of the life of Christ in the *Tertia Pars*). The
separation between dogmatics and morals runs counter to the
letter and spirit of the *Summa*. Curiously, they connect the study
of the sacraments with morality, but the reflective questions that
this connection provokes are treated with such "scholastic precision" that the discussion quickly dissolves into casuistry. As
Thomas Deman, a true conoisseur of the works, points out, their
theological method is not perceived in its specificity (they do
not treat the first question of the *Summa* on *sacra doctrina*) and
their rational development attains a dialectical refinement that is
difficult to surpass: "they did everything so that this detached
wisdom would become a formidable specialty."

While they do not have the breadth of the authors of the
previous period, those of the seventeenth and eighteenth centuries in the rest of Europe deserve to be better known. In
France (with Contenson, Gonet, Goudin, Massoulié), in Belgium (with Billuart), in Italy (with Maurus and Gotti), in Austria
(with the Benedictines of Salzburg), there appeared works of
sometimes considerable breadth, often spoiled by the polemics
with the philosophism of the time, but which are not without
merit. Their most important contribution was to have maintained a living tradition, often for the good and sometimes for
the bad, a tradition that is seen in the constant re-editions of
Thomas's work. This period counts no less than eight editions of

the complete works, the last being the second edition of Venice (1775–86) prepared by B. de Rossi (known as Rubeis). But it was also the period that saw the beginning of a multiplication of manuals *ad mentem sancti Thomae* (in the spirit of Saint Thomas), which often took too many liberties with respect to Thomas, and which left their not-so-glorious mark on the end of this second period of Thomism as well as on a good part of the period that followed.

The *Summa* in the
Twentieth Century

IT MAY BE SURPRISING TO SAY, but the state of Thomism at the dawn of the twenty-first century is still in part conditioned by the history of the two preceding centuries. Before laying out the current state of affairs, it will be helpful to recall briefly what happened before. It is this task that will allow us to see better the difficulty of isolating the history of the *Summa* from that of the surrounding milieu.

In fact, there is no interruption between the period that we have just described and the one that we will be discussing. In the reform movement of Sébastian Michaelis (1543–1618), masters general and chapters of the Order regularly intervened to stimulate a taste for the intellectual life and to rekindle the Thomistic fervor of the Domincans. In 1757 (and reaffirmed by the Chapters of 1777, 1868, and 1898), Master J. T. Boxadors once again invited his confreres to take up the serious study of the Angelic Doctor. One of his allies, S. Roselli, wrote the influential *Summa philosophiae* (1777–83), the several editions of which went quickly out of print. The Dominicans of the Minerva in Rome followed soon after by adopting the text of the *Summa* as the basis for their courses on theology. Few publications resulted from these courses, but we can mention the *Institutiones apologeticae* of V. Gatti (1811–82), the *Theologia thomistica* of F. Xarrié (1866), and the *Institutiones theologiae ad mentem S. Thomae* of N. Puig (1861–63). Use was certainly made of Thomas's *Summa* in writing them, but it does not occupy a central place.

It is in this milieu, but a bit later, that we should place the Dominican cardinal Tommaso Zigliara (1833–93). Although a philosopher, he became the first president of the Leonine Commission, which Leo XIII founded in order to publish a critical edition of Thomas's works. At the same time, two other editions of the *Opera omnia* were published: one in Parma (1852–73), which duplicates the *Piana* (except for the *Summa*), and one in Paris (Vivès, 1871–80), which is not of the same quality.

The secular clergy and the Jesuits also played an active role in this revival, but especially in the area of philosophy: at Piacenza, with V. Buzzetti (d. 1824) and the Sordi brothers; at Naples, where L. Taparelli d'Azeglio (1793–1862), a philosopher of the natural law, introduced the manual of A. Goudin (reprinted in 1859–60) at the Jesuit College; at Rome, where M. Liberatore founded the *Civiltà Cattolica* (1850). J. Kleutgen (d. 1883), the author of the first draft of *Aeterni Patris*, is renowned for his *Theologie der Vorzeit* and his *Philosophie der Vorzeit* (1853–63), which were inspired by Cano and Suarez and had considerable success. Other well-known theologians of the Roman College (the name then borne by the future Gregorian University) such as J.-B. Franzelin (d. 1886), a man of remarkable erudition, also wanted to take Saint Thomas as their master in the area of speculative theology, but their efforts to reconcile him with Suarez were in vain.

Aeterni Patris and Its Consequences

The flowering of Thomism in the nineteenth century certainly bears witness to the interest that Master Thomas excited but, in retrospect, it should be said that theology was not central among its concerns and, as a consequence, neither was the *Summa*. The Thomistic movement was oriented more toward philosophy and this philosophical orientation was itself understood in the broad sense as a political vision of the world that was in essence conservative, designed to counterbalance the influence of the Enlightenment spread by the French Revolution.

Without spending too much time commenting on this socio-political context, we should bear in mind that it was the background to Leo XIII's encyclical *Aeterni Patris* (1879), which had as its aim the "restoration of Christian philosophy according to Saint Thomas." Wishing to restore the Christian social order, the Pope determined that this could not be done without a common Christian thought that was both solid and supple and that would unite those who were working toward that end.

FIRST FRUITS

The repercussions of the encyclical were both decisive and quick. In Italy, the Roman Academy of Saint Thomas (1879) started a number of publications, and the long active Alberoni College of Piacenza published the first Thomistic scientific journal (*Divus Thomas,* 1880). The Saint Thomas College in Rome soon became the Collegio Angelico. From 1924 onwards it published the journal *Angelicum* and later became, in 1963, the University of Saint Thomas.

In Belgium, the chair of Thomistic philosophy, established in 1882 at Louvain by D. Mercier, became (in 1894) an Institute and began publishing the *Revue néoscolastique de philosophie*. At Fribourg in Switzerland, where the Catholic faculty of theology was established in 1889, the teaching of philosophy and theology, entrusted to the Dominicans, would become explicitly Thomistic. In France where, after the disruption caused by the Revolution, the restoration of the Dominican order by Lacordaire allowed the rebirth of Thomism, several journals flourished: the *Revue thomiste* (Toulouse-Fribourg, 1893) and the *Revue des sciences philosophiques et théologiques* (Le Saulchoir, 1907). In Spain, the *Ciencia Tomista* soon followed (Salamanca, 1910); in Germany, *Scholastik* (begun in 1926; became *Theologie und Philosophie* in 1966). The United States also witnessed a similar flourishing. In the area of philosophy, we should point out *The Modern Schoolman* (Saint Louis, 1921), *New Scholasticism* (begun in 1927; became the *American Catholic Philosophical Quarterly* in 1989). In the area of theology, *Theological Studies* (1940) counted a number of eminent Thomists among its contributors and continues to do so. Founded in Washington at the beginning of the twentieth century (in 1905), the first Dominican House of Studies established as its mouthpiece *The Thomist* (in 1939). As its title indicates, this journal is specifically devoted to the study of Thomas. After some uncertain beginnings, difficult moments, and even striking changes in orientation as with many journals, these publications are still alive and well and actively contribute to contemporary philosophical and theological discussions. The appearance of an English edition of *Nova et Vetera* (Ypsilanti, MI, 2003)—a journal originally founded by Charles Journet—which has among its contributors many young students of Thomas, is one of the most recent signs of the continuing vitality of Thomistic studies.

In the absence of more detailed information on the teaching

practices in various places, it is impossible to be more specific about the exact place of the *Summa* in these new initiatives. What is certain is that the commission Leo XIII, assisted by Zigliari, established to publish a critical edition of the *Summa,* quickly began its work. The nine volumes of the *Summa* (along with Cajetan's commentary and a *Supplement*) were published from 1888 to 1906 (the *Summa contra Gentiles* followed only later: 1918–33). What is also certain is that Pius X, worried that the influence of Modernism might undermine Leo XIII's work, established on June 29, 1914, that "the text itself" of the *Summa* should serve as the basis for teaching in pontifical universities.

This intervention was but the first in a series of attempts to impose, in an authoritarian way, Thomas's doctrine. The best known example occurred in 1916 when the Congregation for Studies recommended the adoption of a list of twenty-four philosophical theses that supposedly expressed Aquinas's authentic teaching. They had been submitted to the Congregation for its approval two years prior and were written by a Jesuit (G. Mattiussi). But, as J. A. Weisheipl noticed, twenty-three of them opposed positions taken by Suarez. Quickly, the Jesuit General obtained from Pope Benedict XV the assurance that there was nothing obligatory about the list and that one was free to disagree with its points until they were submitted for further discussion (cf. H. Denzinger, nos. 3601–24). Nonetheless, the obligation to teach according to the method, doctrine, and principles of Saint Thomas was inscribed in the Code of Canon Law promulgated in 1917 (no. 1366 § 2).

What a strange reversal of fortunes! Resisted at its birth, and even condemned, Thomism, once made official, became a weapon in the hands of the authorities. There is nothing all that exceptional in this: any number of such reversals are known to history. But the consequences here were disastrous. Imposed in an authoritarian way, Thomas's doctrine had nothing left of the creative force of the original. The Thomism that was diffused in the manuals no longer referred to Thomas except by the intermediary of second-rate commentators. Rarely sensitive to the biblical and patristic sources (held under suspicion because of anti-Modernism), and imbued with a rationalism of which they were unaware, their authors propagated a repetitious, narrow, and legalistic doctrine that was Thomist only in name. This explains the discredit into which Master Thomas fell in our own century.

RENEWAL

The movement started by Leo XIII had still other results, however. Since philosophy was the special concern of the Pope, we should first take a quick look at this domain, where important thinkers were capable of demonstrating the fruitfulness of research guided by Master Thomas. Two of the most famous French thinkers were Jacques Maritain (1882–1973) and Etienne Gilson (1884–1978). The speculative Thomism of the former was based on the great commentators (especially John of St. Thomas), while the latter, more of a historian, sharply criticized the commentators for betraying Thomas's thought. Both Maritain and Gilson were laymen who assembled around themselves likeminded thinkers (in Canada and the United States especially) and who, without intending to, provoked a declericalization, both of Thomism and, more broadly, of medievalism. Of course, they were not the only ones; they, too, had their teachers. But it was mostly due to their influence that we owe an effective presence of Thomas in the philosophical thought of North America. Still, we can ask ourselves if, because of a lack of a more systematic and deeper study of the texts of Master Thomas, their influence remains largely restricted.

As far as theology is concerned, Pius X's directive that the "text itself" of Thomas should be studied was faithfully followed, at least in the Dominican Houses of Study. The custom of commenting on the text of *Summa* article by article for four years persisted almost until the Second Vatican Council. Certainly there were different nuances: some, of a more speculative orientation, were closer to the tradition of the great commentators; others, more historically oriented, were more interested in the contemporary medieval context and Thomas's sources. But the borders between these two currents were not that rigid: the historical renewal was no stranger to the speculative orientation, nor were speculative concerns unknown to historical research.

This dual interest was remarkably demonstrated in theology and in the related areas of apologetics and mystical theology by the Dominicans Ambroise Gardeil *(Le Donné révélé et la Théologie,* 1909; *La Structure de l'âme et l'Expérience mystique,* 1926) and Reginald Garrigou-Lagrange *(Dieu,* 1914; *De revelatione,* 1918; *Perfection chrétienne et contemplation,* 1923), both of whom were heavily influenced by the great commentators. We should also mention several authors of either dogmatic or moral manuals of theology, with a special mention going to Charles Journet (1891–1975), the author of a monumental work on ecclesiology. As for commentators on the *Summa,* we should give highest mention to Santiago Ramirez (1891–1967; Rome and Fribourg) or to M.-Michel Labourdette (1908–90; Saint-Maximin and Toulouse).

Under the impetus of P. Mandonnet (1858–1936)—who, after leaving Fribourg, established the Thomist Society there in

1926—the Dominican school of the Saulchoir (then at Kain in Belgium) was at the origin of a historical and critical Thomism which continues to expand and to bear fruit at the beginning of the twenty-first century. M.-D. Chenu (1895–90), a friend of Gilson and a collaborator of Mandonnet whose work he continued, and Y. Congar (1904–95) are the most well-known representatives of the school of the Saulchoir. Concerning the question so closely connected to the project of the *Summa* of the nature of theology, we must recall in a special way the work of Chenu (*La théologie au XIIIe siècle,* 3rd ed., 1957) and Congar (s.v. "Théologie" in the *Dictionnaire de théologie catholique,* 1947; *Le Sens de "l'économie salutaire dans la "théologie" de S. Thomas,* 1958; *Tradition et "sacra doctrina" chez S. Thomas,* 1963). To these, we should add the work of M.-R. Gagnebet (*La Nature de la théologie spéculative,* 1938). These works, which were decisive in restoring the exact notion of Thomas's *sacra doctrina,* stressed two fundamental options: the unity of theology requires that there be no separation between the diverse branches (speculative and positive, dogmatic and moral); the aim of theology is not to reach conclusions through a deductive method, but to understand the articles of faith that are the basis of theology. Today, my own research continues in this vein (in addition to the titles cited in the bibliography, see J.-P. Torrell, *Recherches thomasiennes,* 2000).

A good example of this type of renewed approach—and the only one of its kind in the twentieth century to my knowledge—is that of Ghislain Lafont, *Structure et méthode dans la "Somme théologique" de saint Thomas d'Aquin* (1961, reprinted in 1996). The author follows step-by-step the pattern of the *Summa,* while remaining attentive both to its overall structure and to that of each treatise. While it is not a commentary properly speaking, it does allow the reader an opening to the meaning of the work and is today still an excellent introduction to Master Thomas's theological enterprise.

TRANSLATIONS

The most telling sign of the interest raised by the *Summa* in the twentieth century is without a doubt the publication of annotated bilingual editions in the major Western languages. The dean of these translations in actual circulation is the French edition called the "Revue des Jeunes" edition. The first volume was published in 1925 and the series was completed only after the Council. Its seventy-eight volumes offer not only the text in translation, but abundant and precise commentaries, of uneven quality, as is the case with all collected works. Many authors, often prestigious ones such as A.-D. Sertillanges, contributed to it, as well as other fine scholars (H.-F. Dondaine for the Trinity; Ch.-V. Héris and P. Synave for Christology; S. Pinckaers for human acts; J. Tonneau for the law; H.-D. Gardeil, A. Patfoort, and a number of others). This collected work is a remarkable witness to the vitality of Thomism in the French-speaking world between the two wars. Even though long out of print, these volumes have been republished since 1997, and a few of them, somewhat outdated in language and in the commentary, are slated to be redone in order to be brought into line with the best of them. For example, S. Pinckaers has completely redone the volume "Béatitude" (Ia IIae q. 1–5) and I have begun work on a new edition with translation and notes of the volumes *Christologie: Le Verbe incarné* (IIIa q. 1–26; 3 vols., 2002) and *Le Verbe incarné en ses mystères* (IIIa q. 27–59; 5 vols., 2003–4). Other volumes are in the process of being redone. I should point out that a new French translation of the *Summa* has been published with shorter annotations (in four volumes, without *Supplément,* from 1984–86).

Lest I toot too much the French-speaking horn, I should at least mention editions in other languages. The bilingual edition in German, begun in 1933, comprises thirty-six volumes, and is still not complete. Like the French edition, it too has assembled a host of collaborators of great quality (H. U. von Balthasar to name but one). O. H. Pesch has just published the volume on sin (*Die Sunde,* Die deutsche Thomas Ausgabe, vol 12, 2003). The bilingual edition in Spanish, published in sixteen volumes beginning in 1947, benefited from a contest of the best Thomists of the Iberian peninsula, among whom is J. Ramirez. It was replaced by a new edition in Spanish only, with brief introductions, for a more popular audience (1988–94). The bilingual edition in English, begun only during the Council in 1963, was prepared quickly, and its sixty volumes, with brief commentaries, have all already been published. Finally, I should mention the bilingual edition in Italian whose thirty-three volumes appeared in the years 1969–70 and were re-edited in 1980.

The care taken to facilitate access to Thomas's work for a larger public has also encompassed the *Summa contra Gentiles,* which appeared in a bilingual French edition under the care of the Dominicans of Lyons (four volumes, published between 1951–61). The first volume, but the last published, contains a lengthy introduction by R.-A. Gauthier who stands out in the history of Thomistic studies. He also wrote the new *Introduction* (in 1993) which complements and corrects the first without rendering it otiose. Benefiting from the advice and counsel of

R.-A. Gauthier concerning the Latin text, a university team
(Cyrille Michon, Vincent Aubin, Denis Moreau) published a
new and richly annotated translation of the *Summa contra Gentiles* in a widely circulated collection. This is testimony to the renewed interest in this text among circles that were, until now,
barely acquainted with Thomas's work (4 vols., Garnier-Flammarion, nos. 1045–48 [Paris, 1999]). The translation of the *Summa contra Gentiles* into other languages (German, English, Spanish, and Italian) bears witness to the interest in this other *Summa*
by Thomas. I should also point out as worthy of special mention
the unedited and complete bilingual Latin-Italian edition of the
Commentary on the Sentences in ten large volumes (Edizioni Studio Domenicano, Bologna, 1999–2002).

VATICAN II AND ITS IMMEDIATE AFTERMATH

I have already pointed out that most seminaries did not have the
level of culture needed to read Thomas. The *Summa* was merely
a prestigious name; the theology of the manuals presented only a
pale reflection of it. The obligation to study what was perceived
as an ideology incited a veritable reaction of rejection on the
part of those who did not share it. Saint Thomas was thus
spurned on the basis of a doctrine that was no longer really his.

Still, if we recall that a number of experts assisting the bishops came from religious orders (Dominican and Jesuit especially) that had a more careful and ambitious formation in St.
Thomas's teaching than others, we can appreciate the fact that
many of the great architects of Vatican II were Thomist in inspiration (there were some fifty Dominican experts at the Council). Thus the rejection of Thomas did not affect the Council itself. On the contrary, while the Council, in speaking of
theological formation, recommended a return to biblical and

patristic sources, it also desired to bring to light a deeper understanding of the mysteries of salvation. For this to occur, it was important to "grasp their inner coherence by a speculative reflection with Saint Thomas as the master" (*Optatam totius* 16). The new Code of Canon Law, promulgated by John Paul II in 1983, directly quoted the recommendation of the Council (Canon 252). While the obligation had disappeared, the name of Thomas retained its status.

While the years following the Council could leave one with the impression that Thomism was dead and buried, the celebration of the seven hundredth anniversary of Thomas's death in 1274, was marked by meetings of several congresses and the appearance of a number of publications that, on the contrary, showed its continued vitality. To cite but one example: the Pontifical Academy of Saint Thomas began a new collection, "Studi tomistici," which, by 2000, had already published sixty-five titles. The bibliography prepared by Richard Ingardia (Bowling Green, OH, 1993) contains three thousand five hundred entries for the period 1977 to 1990. Not all of these studies are on the *Summa*, nor are they all of equal interest. As is well known, celebrations of someone's prestige are frequently the occasion of performances having more to do with panegyrics than with scholarly contributions, and too many publications lack both rigor and originality. But there are also a number of works of quality.

THOMISM AND MEDIEVALISM

One of the most lasting legacies of the encyclical *Aeterni Patris* has been the revival of historical and critical research concerning not only the *Summa* and its author, but the whole milieu in which it was born. The renewal of medieval studies, evident to some degree throughout Europe, has also aided our understanding of the *Summa*. Of all of the authors I could name in this regard, let me mention the following intellectual giants, who worked indefatigably as editors of the original manuscripts indispensable for a precise understanding of the age: H. Denifle (d. 1905), F. Ehrle (d. 1934), P. Mandonnet (d. 1936), M. Grabmann (d. 1949), P. Glorieux (d. 1979). Even though their work has long been without noticeable effect on speculative theologians, and even if their work has occasionally been rendered obsolete and is often in need of correction, nonetheless the work of these pioneers was critical.

The work of the Leonine Commission, little known to the public at large but highly appreciated in scholarly circles, stands in the background of all of this work. The aim of this organization, established at the request of Leo XIII, was to provide an edition of the works of Thomas comparable to the work he saw being done in France under the impetus of the Charter schools, or in Germany with the *Monumenta Germaniae historica*. The first editors, pressed too quickly by the Pope, who wanted immediate results, were not able to give the two or three first volumes of the edition the attention they would have liked (in fact, the first volume was redone in 1989). But now the publications are of exceptional quality. Beginning in 1952, the Leonine Commission, under the impetus of the General Chapter in Washington (1949) and the Master of the Order, Emmanuel Suarez (d. 1954), then under the direction of P.-M. Contenson (d. 1976), its president from 1964, and largely due to the genius of the general editor, J. Perrier (d. 1981), took on new life and published more than twenty volumes over a short period of time. In addition, the formation of a film library, the fruit of years of microfilming the works of Thomas (as well as many other medieval authors), provided the scholarly world with an incomparable database.

The Leonine edition, a collective work, is the fruit of the work of collaborators too numerous to mention here. What follows are the names of the most well known. In the first generation, Constant Suermondt (d. 1925), the general editor of the *Summa* (1888–1906) and J.-P. Mackey (d. 1935), editor of the *Summa contra Gentiles* (1918–30) are especially remembered. Since the resumption of the work in 1952, the names of note include Antoine Dondaine (d. 1987), who published the *De veritate;* Hyacinthe Dondaine (d. 1987), who brought to completion the four volumes of *Opuscula;* René-Antoine Gauthier (d. 1999), who published, among other things, the *Sententia libri Ethicorum,* the *Sententia libri De anima,* and the *Quodlibeta;* P.-M. Gils (d. 2001), to whom we owe the *De malo,* the *Super Boetium De Trinitate* and other works as erudite as they are fascinating on the autographs of Saint Thomas Aquinas; L.-J. Bataillon who, in collaboration with B.-G. Guyot, was the artisan of the research and reproduction of microfilm copies of the manuscripts and who also collaborated on many of the other volumes, although he seems to have signed his name only to the one on the *Politics.*

I provide this summary list not simply to render homage to these little known and little honored scholars, but also to underscore the irreplaceable nature of their work. Textual criticism and all of the sciences necessary to the establishment of a critical text contribute, first and foremost, to reconstituting the *true text* of Saint Thomas. To give the reader an idea of what this represents let me just say that before the publication of the *De veritate* of the Leonine edition, the text of the then current editions contained no less than ten thousand variants more or less seriously at odds with the original. To ignore this work would be to practice a fundamentalist approach to Thomas's text. We have known for a long time that fundamentalism is a heresy with respect to the Bible. If we can speak of heresy in scholarship, then the term is applicable to reading the *Summa*. It is not a question simply of being mistaken about the true text; it is a question of failing to understand the intention and the actual thought of the author himself.

The Current State of Affairs

If we leave to the scholars the erudition of the Leonine edition which, by definition, cannot reach a large audience, there remains nonetheless a fairly large body of serious historical works that are more accessible. It is important to review these indispensable tools for a reading of the *Summa* that is not too naïve.

PUBLICATIONS

In the first place, and not only in chronological order, is M.-D. Chenu's *Introduction à l'étude de saint Thomas d'Aquin* (1950). This book, which Alain de Libera called "without equal," has influenced generations of medievalists, be they historians, philosophers, or theologians, and has renewed their approach to Saint Thomas. Its effort to resituate Master Thomas within his milieu, not only historically and doctrinally, but also evangelically and theologically, was without precedent, and Chenu shares his own intimate knowledge with great warmth.

Apart from the strictly biographical book by A. Walz, *Saint Thomas d'Aquin* (1962; French adaptation by P. Novarina from the original German), Chenu's book, which was translated into

English under the title *Towards Understanding St. Thomas* (Chicago, 1964), reigned supreme for twenty-five years. Other works in English designed to facilitate an understanding of Thomas's work preceded and accompanied it, for example, Walter Farrell's *A Companion to the Summa* (New York, 1941–42), which summarizes and presents the whole of the *Summa* in four volumes and in a very agreeable style. Additional works that appeared in the United States at this time can be found in Th. F. O'Meara's bibliography, about which I will speak later. For the moment, I will mention only the most recent and important works. A special place must be reserved for J. A. Weisheipl's *Friar Thomas d'Aquino: His Life, Thought, and Works* (New York, 1974), which had the benefit of the most up-to-date research, unknown to Chenu, and which finally provided us with a complete scientific biography. Its success was such that a second edition was published (Washington, 1983) in which the author made a number of corrections and added supplementary material, making it the reference book for the life of Saint Thomas for many years. Mention should also be made of Simon Tugwell's quality work, *Albert and Thomas. Selected Writings* (1988), also in English, which contains not only an excellent biographical introduction but also a good selection of texts in translation. First published in German, O. H. Pesch's book *Thomas von Aquinas. Grenze und Grösse mittelaltericher Theologie* (Mainz, 1988; 3rd ed. 1995) certainly makes use of the *Summa* but does not present its entirety. Rather, Pesch places Aquinas in dialogue with Luther on particular points. If this book does not serve the purpose of an introduction to Thomas, Pesch's approach is original, and he makes many points that the attentive reader will find intriguing.

Allow me also to mention my own book: *Saint Thomas*

Aquinas: The Person and His Work (Washington, 1996). This book first appeared in French (*Initiation à saint Thomas d'Aquin,* 1993; 2nd ed., 2002; 2nd English ed., Washington, 2005) and was subsequently translated into several languages (German, Italian, Portuguese, Spanish). More up-to-date and complete than Chenu's and Weisheipl's, it was conceived as much to make the person of the saint and theologian better known as to provide an introduction to his work. The chapter on the *Summa* complements what I have said here (chapters 2 and 3), by recalling what we know concerning the circumstances of its writing and what the various opinions of scholars are concerning its structure. The other chapters present Master Thomas's various works in the order in which they appeared during his life. This first volume was followed by a second: *Saint Thomas Aquinas: Spiritual Master* (Washington, 2003; in French: *Saint Thomas d'Aquin, Maître spirituel,* 1996; 2nd ed., 2002; also translated into Italian and Polish; the Portuguese translation is in progress). This volume is the doctrinal complement to the first, adding what could not be said in the first volume. Without being totally based on the *Summa,* since it makes use of many of Master Thomas's other writings, the book has the *Summa* clearly in the background of its structure. It seems possible to say that these two books (originally conceived as one) represent the best overall introduction available today.

I must draw attention to other works in the English language that have a rather different point of view. Brian Davies's *The Thought of Thomas Aquinas* (published in 1992) follows the *Summa* rather closely, but without respecting either its order or the respective weights of each part. More attentive to the metaphysical dimension and to rational argument, Davies devotes eleven of his seventeen chapters to questions raised in the *Prima Pars,* while three only are given over to a discussion of the *Secunda Pars* and four to the *Tertia Pars.* Whatever may be the quality of this work, it should be noted that it is not even materially precise and that, as a result, it presents Thomas's thought unevenly. Davies's insistence on the "pure philosophy" that we can extract from Aquinas's works and which is found in a second Davies volume, *Aquinas* (London, 2002), is characteristic of a tendency shared by a number of English language authors who read Thomas from the perspective of analytical philosophy. It is not the place here to debate this kind of approach, but I fear that it misrepresents Master Thomas's real intention and leads to an impasse.

It should be pointed out, however, that there is a growing tendency to recognize and to give due place to the properly theological character of Thomas's work. This perspective, which is at once historical, theological, and spiritual, and which has been so familiar to European audiences for some twenty years, has recently made a foray into the English-speaking world. We can see a little of this in Aidan Nichol's *Discovering Aquinas: An Introduction to His Life, Work and Influence* (London, 2002), and even more in Nicholas M. Healy's *Thomas Aquinas: Theolgian of the Christian Life* (Aldershot, 2003). This approach is gaining favor in North America as well. We have a first witness of this in Th. O'Meara's *Thomas Aquinas: Theologian,* whose appearance (Notre Dame, 1997) was something of an event in the U.S. publishing world. While philosophical thought inspired by Thomas was still alive and well in the United States (the legacy of Gilson and Maritain), the same cannot be said for his theological thought, which has only recently been freed from the yoke of

Neothomism. Certainly there were good theological studies on specific points, but one had to search high and low for one that presented the whole of Thomas's theological thought. This is precisely the advantage of O'Meara's book, which is based almost entirely on the *Summa*. While quite up-to-date on contemporary studies of Thomas, O'Meara approaches them with a well-informed and critical eye.

O'Meara's book is a sign of the times. Insofar as a foreign observer can look at another country with sufficient clarity, it seems to me that the appearance of a new generation of Thomistic theologians, among whom are several lay university professors (is this a sign of a failure on the part of the clergy?), could be a decisive event for the beginning of the twenty-first century. While still not numerous, these new Thomists have already made their mark with a number of publications. By way of example, I should point out one work that offers itself as general introduction: J. Wawrykow and R. van Nieuwenhove, eds., *The Theology of Thomas Aquinas* (Notre Dame, 2004). There is not enough space to list the countless other works on particular themes that have appeared in recent years; nonetheless I would like to mention a few additional works that are signs of this new approach. M. Levering and M. Dauphinais's *Reading John with St. Thomas Aquinas: Theological Exegesis and Speculative Theology* (Notre Dame, 2004) highlights the scriptural character of Thomas's theology. I would also like to point out three works of particular interest: in the area of Christology, P. Gondreau's *The Passions of Christ's Soul in the Theology of St. Thomas Aquinas* (Münster, 2002), from which great profit can be gained; in Trinitarian theology, G. Emery (who is not American, but Swiss!), already known for his book *La Trinité créatrice* (Paris, 1995), one of the most important books of the Thomistic revival, has just published in the United States a book that I recommend to anyone who wishes to understand the way in which Thomistic theology functions in dialogue with contemporary theology, *Trinity in Aquinas* (Ypsilanti, MI, 2003).

Returning to Europe: In spite of numerous publications in Italy on the medieval period, one can only find a small number of works on the *Summa* and its theology. The most notable are no doubt those of I. Biffi who has collected and published a number of previously published articles after reworking them. Among them *I misteri di Cristo in Tommaso d'Aquino* (Milan, 1994) is the first of a series, whose third volume has been published under the title *Teologia Storia e Contemplazione in Tommaso d'Aquino* (Milan, 1995). We are still awaiting the publication of the second volume which, like the first, will treat of the "mysteries" of the life of Christ. The originality of this enterprise in dealing with a part of the *Summa* that is usually ignored (IIIa q. 27–59) deserves recognition. It was this perspective that guided the works of R. Lafontaine (*La Résurrection et l'exaltation du Christ chez Thomas d'Aquin* [Rome, 1983]), of G. Lohaus (*Die Geheimnisse des Lebens Jesu in der Summa theologiae des heiligen Thomas von Aquin* [Freiburg im Breisgau, 1985]), and of L. Scheffczyk ("Die Stellung des Thomas von Aquin in der Entwicklung der Lehre von den Mysteria Vitae Christi," in *Renovatio et Reformatio* [Münster, 1985], pp. 44–70). I myself have finished a similar kind of project, published in two volumes under the title *Le Christ en ses mystères: La vie et l'oeuvre de Jésus selon saint Thomas d'Aquin* (Paris, 1999).

In this section on publications I have only mentioned various modern translations of the *Summa*. At the risk of going beyond our present concerns, I should mention also that since the 1980s, translations of other works into a number of languages have multiplied tremendously. Without enumerating all of them here, I should remind the reader that these other works of St. Thomas's are the natural milieu in which to read the *Summa*. Following the maxim of his first disciples, Thomas is *sui ipsius interpres* (his own interpreter); this means that the reading of any one of his works, even if it be the most important, always gains by being done in conjunction with the others. This principle is best seen by the number of scientific monographs, sometimes of great value, that are now being published. Increasingly, their authors are taking into account the scriptural commentaries and the patristic sources that have otherwise often been ignored. As examples of the renewed attention given to those forgotten parts or points of the *Summa,* I have already mentioned the interest scholars have recently shown in the Trinitarian character of creation and in the mysteries of the life of Christ. To these causes of scholarly interest I could add virtue ethics as well as the salvific causality of the Resurrection.

I cannot end this section on publications without mentioning the monumental *Index thomisticus,* for which we are indebted to the courageous initiative of the Jesuit Roberto Busa. Busa "computerized" not only the *Summa* but also Thomas's entire corpus, creating an index and concordances of a precision and completeness that are unequaled to this day. Published between 1974–80, those forty-nine large volumes, which were not very convenient to use, are now available on CD-ROM, a move that has greatly facilitated research. Long gone are the times when statistics seemed at times to take the place of thought. This new tool has already begun to show its great potential. The use of the

Internet has also become more frequent. Among the many sites useful for consultation, I would like to mention the one designed by Enrique Alcarón of the University of Navarra and other researchers (www.unav.es/filosofia/alcarón/amicis/ctcorpus.html). In addition to the *Opera omnia,* in an easy-to-search form and with a number of research tools, one can also consult at this site the imposing bibliography regularly updated by D. B. Twetten of Marquette University and D. Berger of Cologne.

THREE INSTITUTIONS

One of the reasons for the endurance of the movement that had its origins in *Aeterni Patris* is the fact that it was able not only to express itself in the journals about which we have already spoken, but also to take shape in institutions that perpetuated its first impulse. Some of those who were established then are still in existence and continue, under various forms, to honor their founding charter. In Rome, the University of Saint Thomas, better known as the "Angelicum," established in 1983 its Saint Thomas Institute, which organizes and publishes specialized colloquia in its collection "Studi" (by 2002, six volumes had already been published). For its part, the Gregorian University began in 1992 a regular course in lexicography and hermeneutics, calling upon computer resources in the service of medieval, and most especially Thomistic Latin. In 1996, the Lateran University announced the creation of an interdisciplinary Chair called "Saint Thomas and Contemporary Thought." The limits of this small book and my lack of information prevent me from making a world tour of the various teaching institutions devoted to Thomistic studies. It would be worthwhile to say something about a number of centers where Thomas Aquinas is honored:

the United States, about which I have just spoken; Germany, which has the Thomas-Institut of Cologne and the Grabmann-Institut in Munich, whose publications regularly enrich our knowledge of Thomas and his work; Spain (in which the study of Thomas had practically disappeared), where the University of Navarra has in the past couple of years made a name for itself with its numerous publications; Poland, where the Thomist Institute of Warsaw has taken on new life under the leadership of Michal Paluch. Because I cannot go on at length, I will give only three examples from among those that are the closest and the best known.

The Faculty of Theology of Fribourg (Switzerland), one of the fruits of the renewal called for by Leo XIII, has, since its founding, won renown in a number of areas. If I limit myself to those theologians who are strictly Thomists, it should suffice to recall F. Marin-Sola (1873–1932), Th. Deman (1899–1954), or the famous J. Ramirez, whose teaching, delivered as a direct commentary of the *Summa,* can rival that of any of the great commentators of centuries past. More recently, a new generation has won renown with a series of publications that present, in a singular way, a high degree of speculative thought, while still remaining attentive to method and to the results of historical and critical research (consult, for instance, the list of volumes of the prestigious "Bibliothèque thomiste," [Paris: J. Vrin], or the collection "Vestigia," [Paris: Cerf]). The reader will find, in an article I wrote that appears in the bibliography ("Situation actuelle des études thomiste"), a nearly complete list of these works and their authors. Let it suffice to say here that, for these researchers, Thomas is first and foremost a theologian and that, if they refuse to consider the *Summa* apart from his other writings, it remains nonetheless a focus of their work.

The *Revue Thomiste,* another institution that has its origins in the renewal of the late nineteenth century, recently celebrated its centenary (1993). Under the direction of S.-Th. Bonino (since 1990), surrounded by an entirely new team of editors, it has taken on a new life marked by several publications among which we should mention the centenary edition itself: *Saint Thomas au XXe siècle* (1994) and the special number *Un maître en théologie: M.-M. Labourdette* (1992), which makes better known the work of the man who for forty years wrote on the text of the *Secunda Pars.* Within the Institut Catholique de Toulouse the same organizers are at the origin of the creation of the Institut Saint Thomas d'Aquin (1994), which has already distinguished itself by a series of impressive colloquia and publications in the *Revue Thomiste: Saint Thomas au XIVe siècle* (1997); *Saint Thomas d'Aquin et le sacerdoce* (1999); *Nature et grâce: une controverse au coeur du thomisme au Xx^e siècle* (2001); *"Veritas":Approches thomiste de la vérité* (2004).

The Thomas Instituut in Utrecht, a relatively more recent foundation, has, for more than twenty years, distinguished itself in the eyes of the Thomistic public by an intense teaching program and quality publications. Ten volumes have been published in the series "Publications of the Thomas Instituut te Utrecht" (Louvain: Peeters). Without discussing all of the volumes, I would like to point out the two most recent: W. G. B. M. Valkenberg's *Word of the Living God. Place and Function of Holy Scripture in the Theology of St. Thomas Aquinas* (2000), significant for the attention it pays to an area that, until recently, has been neglected; P. van Geest, H. Goris, and C. Leget, eds., *Aquinas as Authority* (2002), the title of which alone would have been unthinkable twenty years ago. The Instituut also publishes *Jaarboek,* the twentieth title of which (2002) is *Beatitudo—Thomas en Luther.* English is generally used for these publications, but one can also find works in German and Dutch, and more rarely in French. Let me add that the Instituut's Internet site provides an idea of the center's activities and is also useful to consult, for it regularly publishes interviews with different contemporary Thomistic authors and thus allows one to inform oneself about the direction of current research (www.thomasinstituut.org/).

As incomplete and as fragmentary as they are, these indications provide a good idea of the situation at the beginning of the twenty-first century. In spite of the accumulation of titles, this is not meant to be triumphalist. Among Catholic theologians, the disciples of Saint Thomas are in the minority and their publications are far from equaling in number what appears in the fields of exegesis and history. Outside of certain privileged spots, the places where they teach can be counted on one hand. Had it been more complete, this tour of the landscape that I have just sketched could not have hidden the almost complete absence of Thomists in a number of countries where they were once far more numerous. This observation, resituated in a more nuanced historical context, is not meant to be pessimistic, though. Rather, it corresponds to a reality that has always been less glorious than one would have believed for a time at the beginning of the twentieth century.

Conclusion

CCORDING TO THE AIMS of the French series in which
this book originally appeared, my intention has been to
present to the reader the *Summa theologiae,* its author, its
content, and its fortunes through the ages. As this book was
about an important work that has made its presence felt in the
history of ideas for a little more than seven centuries, this undertaking has not been without a certain temerity and this presentation has had to limit itself to the essentials. In spite of,
or perhaps because of these limits, my conclusions are rather
straightforward.

The simple fact that an author and his work were able to at-
tract both support and opposition for as long as Thomas Aquinas
did with the *Summa* is already a sign that the person is no ordinary one, and neither is the work. Only the Platonic school in
Antiquity, as I said earlier, enjoyed a comparable legacy. It would
be useless to revel in this fact, but we can at least ask ourselves
the reasons for this durability.

The strength itself of the synthesis explains it in part. To as-
sert that it stands out by its rare clarity, rigor, and coherence is
not to revive the naïve theory that saw the *Summa* as the summit
of medieval thought (I have taken pains to underscore its relative
character and all that it owes to other authors, previous and contemporaneous). For all that, the *Summa* is not a monolith and we
can detect in places certain incomplete elements. Nevertheless,

it offers to those who know how to read it the means to extend and even correct Thomas's thought. Like a *non finito* of Michelangelo's, it is no less a masterpiece.

We could perhaps cite other works from the past that are no less forceful but which did not enjoy the same fruitfulness. The "luck" of the *Summa* is that it was a textbook. For weal or for woe, its durability can be explained by the generations of professors and students who read and reread it, pored over it, commented on it, and made it relevant, keeping it alive. Looking at things retrospectively, Master Thomas owes much to his disciples and especially to the Dominican order and to his confreres who either preserved or, on several occasions, took up again a tradition without which Thomas's doctrine would have had only an archeological interest. At the same time, Thomas paid his debt, for he thereby provided the Dominicans the means of a a strong identity.

A strong sense of corporate self-satisfaction was not the sole accompaniment, of course. In adapting and extending Master Thomas's thought in many different ways, his disciples also misunderstood him at times, neglected his own originality, and even betrayed him. Still, Otto Hermann Pesch rightly said that the greatness of Thomism is to have done what needed to be done: to bring Thomas into dialogue with the thoughts of times that were not his. The drama came from the fact that the categories of those times, unconsciously assimilated even by the best of his defenders, falsified the conditions for understanding and appropriating exactly his doctrine. But we cannot say that the contribution of these great commentators was negligible (they deserve to be studied for themselves), and a closer look would perhaps also show the contribution of Neothomism.

We do not have to draw up a list of litigious points (which would be long). Independently of distortions of precise points, it seems that the most common and damaging error was to have considered Thomas first of all as a philosopher and to have believed it possible to isolate certain parts of the *Summa* as "philosophical." This is a glaring error of perspective. The *Summa* is theological from beginning to end and its author is first and foremost a theologian who uses philosophical categories as he has need, but grants them a "foreign and only probable authority" (Ia q. 1 a 8 ad 2) in his synthesis.

In insisting on the need to restore the "philosophy" of Master Thomas, Leo XIII succeeded only in rooting Neoscholaticism in the hypertrophy of this dimension to the detriment of Thomas's formally theological intention. If it is uncontestable that Thomas is a first-rate philosopher, and if there is no question of excluding him from the investigations of his peers, I must insist that the reader also give all of his attention to Thomas as a theologian, a disciple of the Fathers of the Church and an interpreter of the Bible, for Sacred Scripture is already for him as Vatican II wished: "the soul of theology." It is for this reason that one must return to the Master beyond his commentators and here the *Summa* proves itself to be incomparable.

One must always and again return to reading the *Summa* because it is a complete book. First, it is complete in its content, since by its very focus it wants to offer the whole of Christian doctrine synthetically organized. It is complete too, and perhaps especially, in its method, since it contains everything necessary for an integral theological approach: a listening to revealed data in the form of Sacred Scripture, the presence of the tradition by an abundant use of the Fathers of the Church and the great

Councils, a constant attention to the wisdom of philosophers whatever be their origin, and finally a recourse to human experience in all of its complexity. Of course, all of this has to be actualized with the help of current scientific discoveries. This is, in fact, what Thomas did in his own time. But if today's reader conducts himself as a true disciple, trying to reproduce the scientific quest and the spiritual attitude of the Master, he cannot fail, for his part, to gain an exact understanding of the *Summa*.

Annotated Bibliography

THE STYLE OF THIS BOOK does not lend itself to a lot of footnotes or references. Specialists will recognize my sources. But for the non-specialists, here are some references that will help to extend their reading.

For the first chapter, one can find all of the desired information on the life and works of Thomas in J.-P. Torrell, *Saint Thomas Aquinas, vol. 1, The Person and His Work*, Washington, D.C.: C.U.A. Press, 1996 (2nd ed. revised and expanded with a critical updating and bibliography, Washington, D.C.: C.U.A. Press, 2005.

For chapters 2 and 3, see again J.-P. Torrell, *Saint Thomas Aquinas, vol. 2, Spiritual Master*, Washington, D.C.: C.U.A. Press, 2003 (this translation, from the first French edition of *Saint Thomas d'Aquin, Maître Spirituel*, published in 1996, will be complemented by the 2nd ed. revised and expanded with a Postface, Paris-Fribourg, 2002), in which I tried to translate the great intuitions of Thomas's theology in an accessible way for today's reader. One should also refer to the more systematic introduction of A. Patfoort, *La Somme de saint Thomas et la logique du dessin de Dieu*, Saint-Maur: Parole et Silence, 1998.—J.-H. Nicolas's *Synthèse dogmatique. De la Trinité à la Trinité*, Paris-Fribourg, 1985, and *Synthèse dogmatique. Complément: de l'univers à la Trinité*, Paris-Fribourg, 1993 will provide the reader with a more rigorous exposition of the dogmatic part of the *Summa* (First and Third Parts). The theology of the Trinity has been considerably renewed by the work of G. Emery, *La Trinité créatrice* (Paris: J. Vrin, 1995); *Trinity in Aquinas* (Ypsilanti, MI: Sapientia Press, 2003).—For Christology, see Thomas d'Aquin, *Le Verbe incarné*, rev. ed., French translation, notes, and appendices by J.-P. Torrell, 3 vols. (Paris: Cerf, 2002); Thomas d'Aquin, *Le Verbe incarné en ses mystères*, rev. ed., French translation, notes, and appendices by J.-P. Torrell, 5 vols. (Paris: Cerf, 2003–4).

Concerning the moral part of these two chapters, the most complete sustained commentary is that of M.-M. Labourdette, *Cours de théologie morale,* edited in offset by the Dominicans of Toulouse. If this is unattainable, the reader will find a brief presentation of the whole by J.-P. Torrell, "Thomas Aquinas. La 'philosophie' morale" in M. Canto-Sperber, *Dictionnaire d'éthique et de philosophie* morale (Paris: P.U.F., 1996), pp. 1516–23.—For fundamental moral theology *(Prima Secundae),* see S.-Th. Pinckaers, *The Sources of Christian Ethics* (Washington, D.C.: C.U.A. Press, 1995), which is more extensive than a commentary but very close to Thomas's thought. I should also point out the important essay of Denis J. M. Bradley, *Aquinas on the Twofold Human Good. Reason and Human Happiness in Aquinas's Moral Science* (Washington, D.C.: C.U.A. Press, 1997).—To my knowledge, there do not exist comparable works for the *Secunda Secundae,* but you will find S. J. Pope, ed., *The Ethics of Aquinas* (Washington, D.C.: Georgetown University Press, 2002), helpful.

Chapter 4 on the literary and doctrinal milieu of the *Summa* contains information borrowed from a number of specialized studies impossible to list here. The reader will find a helpful, even if a little outdated, description of this context in M.-D. Chenu, *Towards Understanding St. Thomas* (Chicago, 1964). This can be supplemented by reading the corresponding explanations in the *Dictionnaire encyclopédique du Moyen Âge,* under the direction of A. Vauchez, 2 vols. (Paris: Cerf, 1997).

The history of Thomism and of the great commentators treated in chapter 5 also necessitated recourse to a number of works. For an overview, see first of all J. A. Weisheipl's article "Thomism" in the *New Catholic Encyclopedia,* vol. 14, 2nd ed., 2003, 40–52 (it should be noted, however, that apart from additional bibliographical references, the documentation remains essentially that of the 1st ed. in 1967). Unable to list all of the works used, I can at least list some of those that deal with the main moments of this history, which will allow for further study: *Saint Thomas au XIVe siècle,* special number of the *Revue Thomiste* (1997:1), in which the reader will find twelve contributions that considerably renew the approach to this period.—*Jean Capreolus et son temps (1380–1444),* under the direction of G. Bedouelle, R. Cessario, and K. White, Mémoire dominicaine, Cahier spécial 1 (Paris, 1997): eighteen studies that represent an unprecedented contribution to the knowledge of the man, his work, and his philosophical and theological thought; John Capreolus, *On the Virtues,* trans. K. White and R. Cessario (Washington, D.C.: C.U.A. Press, 2001).—P. O. Kristeller, *Le thomisme et la pensée italienne de la Renaissance* (Paris-Montreal, 1967), remains important in order to grasp the continuity that exists between scholasticism and humanism.—S. Swiezawski, "Le thomisme à la fin du moyen Âge" in *Studi tomistici* 1 (1974): 225–48, for a picture of the whole.—On the school of Salamanca, see R. Hernandez Martin, *Francisco de Vitoria. Vida y pensamiento internacionalista* (Madrid: B.A.C., 1995), and the little book by the same author published in French: *Francisco de Vitoria et la "Leçon sur les Indiens,"* Classiques du Christianisme (Paris: Cerf, 1997), in which one can find lengthy passages of this text and follow the traces of his influence; Th. F. O'Meara, "The Dominican School of Salamanca and the Spanish Conquest of America: Some Bibliographical Notes," in *The Thomist* 56 (1992): 555–82.—Cajetan was himself the subject of a colloquium in which one will find the current state of research: B. Pinchard and S. Ricci, eds., *Rationalisme analogique et humanisme théologique*(Naples: Vivarium, 1993).—C. Fabro, "Il posto di Giovanni di San Tommaso nella scuola tomistica," in *Angelicum* 66 (1989): 56–90.—Th. Deman, "Salamanque (Théologiens de)" in *Dictionnaire de théologie catholique* 14 (Paris: Letouzey et Ané, 1939), 1017–31.—Given the close connection between the fate of Thomism and that of the Dominicans, it is useful to know W. A. Hinnebusch, *The Dominicans. A Short History* (New York: Alba House, 1975), in which almost every chapter contains a paragraph or two on intellectual life in the Order.—Finally, we should add the complementary book of another Dominican, R. Cessario, *A Short History of Thomism* (Washington, D.C.: C.U.A. Press, 2005).

For the history of the renaissance of Thomism (chapter 6), see J. A. Weisheipl, s.v., "Scholasticism: 3. Contemporary Scholasticism" in *New Catholic Encyclopedia,* 2nd ed., vol. 12, 772–79 (the documentation is dated); G. A. McCool, *Nineteenth-Century Scholasticism. The Search for a Unitary Method* (New York: Fordham University Press, 3rd ed., 1999); *The Neo-Thomists* (Milwaukee: Marquette University Press, 1994); R. Aubert, *Aspects divers du néothomisme sous le pontificat de Léon XIII* (Rome, 1960); Jon Alexander, "Aeterni Patris: 1879–1979. Bibliography of American Responses" in *The Thomist* 48 (1979): 480–81.—This can be supplemented with M. Regnier, "Le thomisme depuis 1870," pp. 483–500 in Y. Belaval, ed., *Histoire de la Philosophie*, vol. 3 (Paris: La Pléiade, 1984).—E. Villanova, "Léon XIII et le néothomisme," pp. 605–21 in E. Villanova, ed., *Histoire des théologies chrétiennes*, vol. 3. (Paris, 1997), is more interested in the political than the philosophical or theological aspects.—P.-M. de Contenson, "Documents sur les origines et les premières années de la Commission Léonine," pp. 331–88 in *St. Thomas Aquinas. 1274–1974. Commemorative Studies*, vol. 2 (Toronto, 1974), is very instructive on the first years of the Commission.—Before and after Vatican II, the reader will find a lot of information in the following titles: G. Prouvost, ed., *Étienne Gilson—Jacques Maritain, Correspondance 1923–1971* (Paris, 1991); *Autour d' Étienne Gilson. Études et documents*, special no. of the *Revue Thomiste* (1994:3); *Un Maître en théologie. Le Père Marie-Michel Labourdette*, special no. of the *Revue Thomiste* (1992:1); *Saint Thomas au XXe* under the direction of S.-Th. Bonino (Paris, 1994).—As for recent developments, you can find more details in J.-P. Torrell, "Situation actuelle des études thomistes" in *Recherches de science religieuse* 91 (2003): 343–71.

Index

Aquinas's Summa: *Background, Structure, & Reception* was designed and composed in
Bembo with Centaur display by Kachergis Book Design of Pittsboro,
North Carolina. It was printed on 60-pound Natural Offset
and bound by McNaughton & Gunn, Inc.,
of Saline, Michigan.